MAKE YOUR OWN
contemporary
QUILTS

# MAKE YOUR OWN
## contemporary QUILTS

photography by
**paola pieroni**

HACHETTE Illustrated

# Contents

Introduction                          6
Tools                                 8
Materials                            14

## Quilt projects                    20

Rose constellations                  22
Art Deco abstract                    26
French knots on navy                 30
Sea of dreams                        34
Pompom maze                          38
Bejewelled seams                     42
Liberty's song bird                  46
Gumleaves                            50
Guardian angels                      54
White romance                        58
Cocoon                               62
Spirit of Ndebele                    66
Forms of attachment                  70
Tasselbrick                          74
Earthspring                          78
Oxfam flowers                        82
Desert dreaming                      86
Cappuccino waves                     90
Machiko's gift                       94
Poppy fields                         98

## Techniques and templates         104

Estimating yardage                  106
Preparing the fabric                109
Sewing skills and stitches          110
Pressing                            117
**Patchwork**
Making templates                    118
Marking out the fabric              119
Cutting out patchwork
   pieces                           120
Piecing patchwork                   123
**Appliqué**
Patterns and templates              128
Preparing the fabrics               129
Applying appliqué                   131
**Quilting**
Quilting patterns                   135
Preparing the fabrics               137
Quilting                            139
**Finishing the quilt**
Attaching bindings                  143
Personalising your quilt            144
Making a hanging sleeve             145
Taking care of your quilt           145
**Templates**                       146

Contributors                        156
Index                               158

# Introduction

We all know how much impact colour and pattern have on the interior design of our homes, but in the last few years we have also come to really value the extra depth and pleasure that texture can contribute. Successful contemporary interiors tend to feature layers of texture that are built up with natural materials, which might include wood, cane, ceramics, stone – and, of course, fabric. If you have followed this trend and have a love of needlework and fabric art, your thoughts will naturally have focused on the beautiful home accessories that feature knitted, embroidered, beaded – and quilted – textiles, which are now widely available.

Quilts have been made for centuries, but enjoyed a major revival of interest in the last quarter of the twentieth century. So it's hardly surprising that with today's interest in texture and fabric, and a revival in the appreciation of good craftsmanship, the quilt has been elevated to make a dramatic personal and decorative statement in the contemporary home. That's a long way from the humble beginnings of quilting, when a layer of stuffing was stitched between two pieces of fabric purely to give warmth and provide a practical cover for a bed. However, the decorative scope of the quilt top did not take long to emerge and, even when quilt makers were saving precious scraps of fabric to piece together into patchwork and appliqué, they were also devising wonderful geometric and floral designs that would flood their homes with colour, pattern and texture.

You have the ability to create a beautiful quilt that will add visual impact and tactile appeal to your own home at your fingertips. If you are new to quilting, this book will introduce you to the joys and satisfaction of working with fabric to make a quilt that you can be proud to display as a work of art, not just as a cosy bedspread. If you are a more seasoned quilt maker, you will already appreciate how you can create a quilt with endless possibilities for self-expression to enhance a particular room, but will still find inspiration from the designs here.

The twenty quilts in this book have a broad range of appeal. The international quilt makers who designed them have brought their very different approaches and styles to the project from quite diverse backgrounds. The result is a collection of exciting ideas for quilts to cover beds and cots, use in the garden or make a bold statement on a wall, using traditional and modern techniques. Liberty's Song Bird has a classic border of quarter-square patchwork triangles, while Earthspring and Bejewelled Seams use rotary cutting to best advantage for modern block quilts. Poppy Fields and Spirit of Ndebele show that appliqué can be an art form, born from quite different cultural heritages. Some designs also blur the boundaries between quilting and embroidery. On Sea of Dreams, ribbons are embellished with hand embroidery stitches, while flowing machine quilting secures the cut edges of Gumleaves, and lustrous wool and silk fibres are trapped with free-motion stitches to create a totally new surface for Cocoon. Other designs stretch our understanding of the quilt form even further. Desert Dreaming and Pompom Maze both leave frayed edges to dramatically different effect and fabric is manipulated into deep folds in Cappuccino Waves and gorgeous flowers in Rose Constellations.

Whether you are new to quilting or have years of experience, you will find a wealth of inspiring ideas in *Contemporary Quilts*. Once tempted, beginners can rely on the advice for selecting tools and materials at the front of the book and the essential techniques at the back will be an invaluable reference for everything they need to know. All the templates for the quilt designs are also provided.

Discover the joy and excitement of making a beautiful quilt to add style to your home. You never know – you might become hooked for life on this very rewarding pastime!

# Tools

You don't need many specialist tools to make quilts and if you already do some sewing, you will probably be well equipped. If you become hooked by patchwork, as many people do, you might like to invest in a rotary cutter, quilter's ruler and cutting mat so that you can cut lots of shapes quickly and accurately. None of these tools are difficult to obtain if you do need to buy them – look in good haberdashers, specialist quilting and art supply shops and at mail order details in magazines and on the Internet. Buy the best you can afford to keep your measuring and cutting absolutely accurate.

## TOOLS FOR TEMPLATES AND PATTERNS

### Lead pencil
A propelling pencil is useful for making tracings of templates and patterns onto paper. It can also be used for marking fabric where the marks will not be seen. An ordinary lead HB pencil will do the same job, but keep the point sharpened.

### Tracing paper
Tracing paper is excellent for making tracings of design outlines and patterns from books and magazines. The tracing can then be transferred to card or plastic to make templates. You can substitute greaseproof (waxed) paper for the same task. It is cheaper and comes in long lengths, but it is not as transparent as tracing paper.

### Permanent fine-line marker
A permanent black marker gives a strong outline to patterns so that they can be traced easily through fabric. Also use one for labelling templates and for signing your name on the back of your quilt. Never use a ball-point pen instead because the ink will invariably smear and is impossible to get rid of.

### Drafting triangle
Although you could use a quilt ruler instead, a large, right-angled drafting triangle is invaluable for making sure that lines are perpendicular to each other. This is essential when drawing your own templates or straightening the edges of your fabric.

### Metal ruler
Use a long metal ruler for marking and checking straight lines, but never use one with a rotary cutter because it will blunt the blades. A metal ruler may be a suitable width for marking out parallel quilting lines.

### Computer
Whether you use the most basic software for drafting geometric templates or more specialist packages for designing the patchwork or appliqué on whole quilt tops, a computer can be an invaluable and inspiring tool. Of course, it is not essential to use one.

### Template plastic
Sheets of template plastic, available with a printed grid or without, are well suited to making templates because you can trace the template pattern through the plastic and see the pattern on fabric through it. The plastic is also very durable. It can be cut with scissors, although it is a good idea to cut roughly around the shapes first and then cut very carefully along each outline because the plastic can be awkward to manoeuvre.

### Card
Firm card that can be cut with scissors or a craft knife makes perfectly acceptable templates, although it is not as durable as template plastic. It can also be used to give temporary stability to appliqué shapes.

### Craft knife

Make sure that your craft knife always has a sharp blade for cutting out card templates accurately and keep a stock of spare blades handy.

### Paper scissors

A sharp pair of paper scissors will cut card and template plastic if you don't have a craft knife. Never use your dressmaker's shears for this purpose.

### Ready-made templates

Plastic or metal templates for popular patchwork shapes and quilting designs are available from quilting shops. Patchwork templates include the finished shape and a matching window template giving the standard seam allowance. This allows you to mark the stitching or the cutting line, or both.

*A selection of tools for making templates and patterns*

### Spray adhesive

Spray adhesive can be used to mount tracings of templates onto card. Always follow the manufacturer's instructions.

### Glue stick

Sticks of water-soluble adhesive provide a convenient way of temporarily fixing appliqué shapes to background fabric before permanently sewing them in place.

### Paper-backed fusible web

Fusible web, with a paper backing, is available in sheets or on a roll from quilting shops and good haberdashers. It bonds one fabric to another and is excellent for giving stability to appliqué shapes. Follow the manufacturer's instructions to iron and fuse one side of the web to the appliqué shape, then peel off the paper backing and fuse the other side of the web to the background fabric.

### Iron-on interfacing

This can be used to give stability to flimsy and lightweight fabrics, particularly for appliqué. Follow the manufacturer's instructions to iron and fuse the adhesive side of the interfacing to the wrong side of fabric.

### Freezer paper

The shiny side of ordinary freezer paper, available from supermarkets, sticks onto fabric when ironed in place without leaving any residue on the fabric or on the iron. Use it to give temporary stability to appliqué shapes – it can be traced through, gives a very crisp edge, and can be removed easily and used repeatedly.

## MEASURING, MARKING AND CUTTING EQUIPMENT

### Tape measure

Only use a flexible tape measure for assessing the basic yardage of fabric or for short measurements in circumstances where a ruler is impossible to use. It is not accurate enough for drafting templates or measuring patchwork pieces.

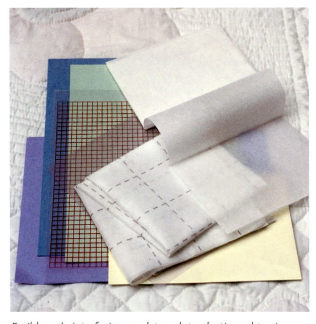

*Fusible web, interfacing, card, template plastic and tracing paper for making templates and patterns*

### Dressmaker's scissors

A pair of good quality scissors is invaluable for cutting fabric, especially for curved shapes if you do not have a rotary cutter. A large pair of shears will make quick work of cutting long lengths of fabric, but a smaller pair is more appropriate for cutting patchwork pieces. Always keep the blades sharp and never use them for cutting paper or plastic.

### Rotary cutter

This effective tool has revolutionized patchwork and quilting. The round blade is rolled against the edge of a quilter's ruler across the fabric to cut strips and simple shapes quickly and accurately. The blades are exceptionally sharp, so make sure that you retract the blade when the cutter is not in use. Keep the cutter and a stock of spare blades in a container, such as a pencil box, out of harm's way.

### Quilter's ruler

This specialist transparent ruler really comes into its own when used with a rotary cutter for measuring and cutting strips and simple shapes. The rulers are clear with a grid marked off at regular intervals and different angles for marking out geometric shapes. They are available in different widths, but a wide, non-slip one is particularly useful.

### Cutting mat

A good quality self-healing cutting mat is essential for use with a rotary cutter to protect the surface underneath. They are available from quilting and art supply shops. If possible, buy a large mat of at least 45 x 60cm (18 x 24in).

### Quilter's quarter

This simple little bar is exactly 6mm ($\frac{1}{4}$in) wide on each side and specifically designed to make easy work of marking out standard allowances along straight lines. A flexi-curve or a little metal quarter wheel, which takes a pencil point in the middle and can be rolled along the edge of a template, can be used to mark allowances around curved shapes.

### Quilter's pencil

These pencils are usually available in white, yellow, silver or blue, so you should always be able to find one that is clearly visible on any colour of fabric. The colour can either be washed out or will eventually wear off the fabric, making the pencils ideal for marking appliqué designs and quilting patterns on the right side of the fabric. Always keep the points sharp.

### Chalk powder wheel

This pencil-shaped tool contains powdered tailor's chalk, which is deposited along the lines made by a tiny serrated wheel, and is excellent for marking sweeping lines, and appliqué and quilting patterns. The colour can be washed out or will eventually wear off the fabric.

### Water-erasable markers

You can use either a light or dark coloured water-erasable marker in order to transfer appliqué and quilting patterns to the right side of the fabric. However, heat sets the ink to become permanent, so do not press the fabric before washing it. Whichever tool you use for marking fabric, first test it on similar fabric to ensure it is suitable for the task. Think about whether it washes out or bleeds, and how quickly it rubs off.

### Light box

A light box is an invaluable tool used for tracing appliqué templates and quilting designs onto any fabric you are using. However, you can also improvise to achieve the same effect by using a glass-topped table with a lamp underneath, or a window.

## SEWING AIDS

### Dressmaker's pins

Long, fine pins are essential for pinning layers of fabric together. Some of them have glass heads, which can make them easier to use, but avoid those with plastic heads because they melt if touched by an iron.

### Needles

Use short, fine needles in sizes 8 to 12 for all hand sewing, piecing patchwork and applying appliqué. Betweens in sizes 8 to 10 are recommended for quilting. It is best to try and use the smallest size in order to keep your stitches tiny and regular. You could use a longer needle for basting.

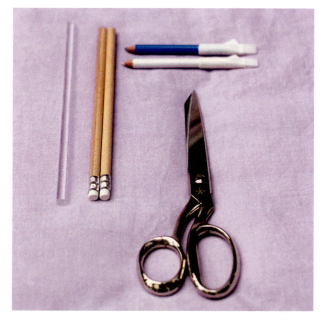

*Dressmaker's scissors, quilter's quarter and tools for marking the fabric*

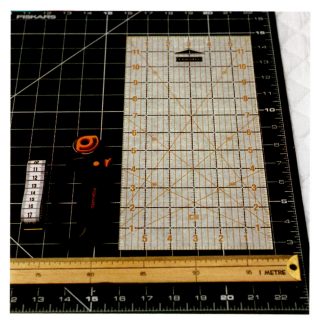

*Rotary cutter and cutting mat, with quilter's ruler and other measuring tools*

### Needle threader

This is an invaluable little tool if you need help to get thread through the eye of a small needle. Push the metal loop on the threader through the needle eye. Pass the thread through the loop and then pull the tool back through the eye to draw the thread with it.

You can also adapt this principle for techniques such as hand tying quilts, by using thin thread to draw thicker yarn through the eye of a bigger needle.

### Thimble

You can choose either a metal or a leather thimble with a flat top, which fits comfortably on the middle finger of your sewing hand. The thimble will then protect the top of your finger as it pushes the needle through the layers of the quilt. It is best to hold the eye of the needle against the side of the thimble. You may also want to protect the index finger on your other hand while quilting because it will often come into contact with the point of the needle.

### Beeswax

Beeswax is available in small cakes and is used to strengthen thread so that it glides through the fabric more easily and does not tangle. Grip the thread at each end and slide it over the surface of the beeswax.

### Embroidery scissors

These small scissors with sharp points are very useful for trimming threads close to the fabric and for clipping into seam allowances. Always keep the blades sharp. Special appliqué scissors are also available that have been designed for cutting through layers of fabric from the back so that the top fabric does not get cut.

### Iron and ironing board

A clean steam iron and a sturdy ironing board are absolutely essential for achieving precision at all stages of patchwork, appliqué and finishing a quilt. A pressing cloth of cotton fabric will also often be needed to protect the quilt fabric. Use a non-stick sheet when pressing fusible web onto fabric to protect your ironing board cover.

### Quilting hoop

A wooden hoop of at least 35cm (14in) diameter is recommended for stretching the fabric for quilting. A simple hoop does the job well, although hoops on stands that leave both hands free for quilting are also available. The rings on a quilting hoop are deeper than those on an embroidery hoop to grip the three layers of a quilt more securely. Many quilters bind the inner ring of the hoop with bias binding to achieve an even better grip.

To stretch the quilt in the hoop, first place the plain ring under the quilt. Position the ring with the screw over the top of the quilt and the bottom ring. Tighten the screw so that the fabric is slightly less than drum tight. Always remove the quilt from the hoop after a quilting session so that the fabric does not become stained by the wood.

### Seam ripper

This tool is very useful for unpicking machine stitches. However, do not be tempted to rip the blade down a seam because this will risk tearing the fabric. Instead, use the seam ripper to cut across stitches at regular intervals. Then pull the bottom thread free and pick off the remaining bits of thread.

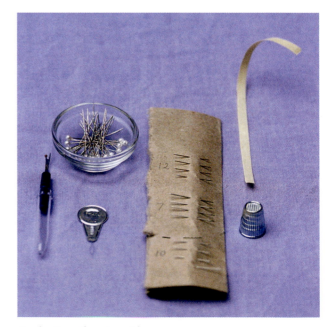

*A selection of sewing aids*

### Masking tape

Use masking tape to keep the layers of a quilt taut until they are being basted or safety pinned together. Some quilters use 6mm (¼in) tape to mark straight lines on the fabric for machine quilting, but you must take care with this method because it is easy to catch the tape with the needle, leaving a sticky residue of adhesive which is then difficult to remove.

### Safety pins

Brass safety pins, 2.5cm (1in) long, are invaluable for securing the layers of a quilt together before machine quilting. They stay securely fixed, unlike ordinary pins that often work loose. Although straight safety pins are fine, curved pins that pick up the layers more easily, are available from specialist shops. As a very general guide you will need about 150 safety pins for a 120 x 150cm (48 x 60in) quilt.

### Sewing machine

Even a very basic sewing machine will make quick work of patchwork, appliqué and quilting. It must have a zigzag facility for appliqué and a choice of various different feet, depending on the technique required. Always use and maintain your machine in accordance with the manual.

*Quilter's hoop, beeswax, embroidery scissors and safety pins*

### Sewing machine needles

Make sure that you have a good supply of needles. They do go blunt or burr and you must use a sharp needle to prevent the fabric snagging. Choose the appropriate size of needle to suit the fabric you are working with – the finer the fabric, the finer the needle you need. Specialist needles for quilting and embroidery are also available. A jeans needle, with an extremely slim point, is good for machine quilting.

### Presser foot

Also called a running foot, this is the basic machine sewing foot and is used for sewing seams in patchwork. It can also be used for sewing close satin stitch around appliqué shapes if a special foot is not needed or available. If your presser foot is exactly 6mm (¼in) from the centre to the edge, you can use it as a gauge for accurate standard seam allowances.

### Walking foot

This attachment is used for quilting because it feeds both the top and bottom layers of fabric through the machine evenly. It is also ideal for use where patterns such as stripes, checks and tartans (plaids) need to be accurately matched at the seams.

### Quilting foot

A quilting foot is just the right width to use as a gauge to give accurate 6mm (¼in) seams. Some also have an adjustable bar attachment that can be used to gauge the even spacing of quilting lines.

### Darning foot

This foot is used for free-motion quilting and machine embroidery, although some machines do not need a foot at all for these methods of sewing.

# Materials

To make a beautiful quilt, you need good quality materials. The fabrics and thread will always be on display, so every choice you make will have an impact on the finished design. Even the type of wadding you choose will add a particular character to your quilt. So select your materials carefully for the very best results.

### Thread

A strong, good-quality thread is essential for quilting. Pure cotton, No 50, is the popular choice and is available in a wide range of colours. Select a colour to match the darkest colour in the fabric or, if you are quilting across lots of different ones, choose a neutral colour, such as ecru or medium grey, which will blend in. Alternatively, you could use monofilament quilting thread for machine appliqué and quilting. This specialist thread is available in clear or smoke and breaks easily when pulled between the fingers (if it did not do so, it would tear through the fabric). In some respects monofilament is not as visible as ordinary thread, but it can be more obvious because it tends to catch the light.

A wider range of threads is suitable for piecing patchwork and appliqué. Choose from pure cotton or cotton-wrapped polyester machine sewing thread, No 40 – or even silk if you are working with silk fabric. You will also need thread for basting and white or off-white will usually be good choices when it comes to removing these stitches.

### Wadding

Hidden from view, but so important to the overall look and feel of the quilt, the choice of wadding can seem quite bewildering. Wadding is available in different materials and thicknesses, or lofts. Since both characteristics determine how well the quilting pattern will be defined and how warm the quilt will be, as well as being quite different to work with, it is worth considering your choice carefully. Wadding comes in different widths and is also available pre-cut to fit the popular bed sizes.

Modern wadding is usually needlepunched or bonded to reduce the tendency of the fibres to migrate through the quilt top and backing. Some types of wadding need to be soaked before layering to shrink them and improve the ease with which they can be quilted; others need fluffing up in a tumble dryer. Whichever type you choose, open the wadding out and allow any folds to relax before you use it. Different types of wadding also have specific requirements as to the closeness of the quilting stitches. So read the product information before you buy to ensure that you make the best choice for your quilt.

The US term 'batting' is also often used for wadding. You will see it particularly in relation to cotton wadding, which is often imported from North America.

### Polyester

A very practical and the least expensive choice, polyester wadding is very readily available in a range of thicknesses, although the thinner, lightweight 70g (2oz) wadding is often recommended for hand quilting. The thicker the wadding, the warmer the quilt will be and yet polyester is light, easy to quilt and simple to wash. However, it is not recommended for use in quilts for babies, because of the risk of the baby overheating.

### Cotton

Cotton wadding drapes well and makes a flatter quilt with an antique look and a more substantial feel. However, it is not as easy to quilt as polyester wadding. It is also heavier, more cumbersome to wash and will shrink if the water is too warm. The cotton has a tendency to bunch up when washed, although needlepunched or bonded varieties reduce this problem. This often allows quilting lines to be spaced up to 10cm (4in) apart, instead of the more cautious 2.5cm (1in) apart, but do read the product information to make sure.

### Wool

Another substantial wadding, wool is available in medium to heavy weights. It is easy to stitch, with the natural lanoline lubricating the needle as you quilt.

### Silk

Silk wadding is easy to quilt because it is thin and lightweight. It is also the perfect partner for silk fabric and thread. It shrinks very little.

### Fabric

The infinite array of fabrics suitable for making quilts conjures up the idea of being in a sweetie shop or an Aladdin's cave – it can seem bewildering and exciting all at the same time!

However, you don't have to buy great quantities of fabric all at the same time or even know exactly what you are going to do with it when you do buy it. Many quilt makers buy a length of fabric they particularly like as and when they see it and add it to their stash of fabric. This gives them a collection of favourite fabrics from which to choose when they want to start their next quilt. Then they can supplement what they need easily by buying shorter quantities especially for a specific project. All specialist quilting retailers will sell short lengths off the bolt. They will also have a stock of pre-cut fat quarters (46 x 56cm or 18 x 22in of fabric) and fat eighths (23 x 56cm or 9 x 22in), which are addictively irresistible and large enough to make a useful contribution to most quilt designs.

Fabric is woven into different widths, often related to the type of fibre used. The most widely available width for pure cotton is 112cm (44in), but silk, for example, might be available in the narrower width of 90cm (36in) or much wider at 137cm (54in). Be aware that the width of the fabric you choose will affect how much you need, so make your calculations carefully.

You will probably want to re-interpret the quilt designs in this book and choose different fabrics or colours to suit your

*Pure cotton quilting thread*

*Pure cotton sewing machine thread*

own requirements, or may even wish to design your own. Obviously you need to consider the fabrics for the quilt top carefully, whether your design is for a whole-cloth quilt or has lots of patchwork pieces or appliqué. But don't forget to consider the binding and backing too. Your choice of fabric for the binding can alter the look of the whole quilt top and if you choose the right backing fabric your quilt can also be used the other way up.

### Types of fabric

The fibres that make up any fabric determine not only the look of the cloth, but also how easy it is to look after. So first consider the purpose of your finished quilt, how much wear that will subject the fabric to and how often it will need laundering. If it is destined for a baby's cot, it will need a lot of washing and pure cotton would be the best choice. You might decide that a quilt for an adult's bed or sofa throw can be dry-cleaned. Although you could select a more exotic fabric, it still needs to withstand a fair amount of wear, so a pure silk or wool might be suitable. If your quilt is to be

displayed on a wall, it will probably need only an occasional shake to dislodge dust and you could use quite fragile fabrics such as organza or velvet.

The way in which the fibres are combined gives the fabric other characteristics. Natural fabrics are woven together, which leaves gaps between the threads and makes them easier to stitch by hand or machine. Closely woven fabrics tend to be more suitable for quilting, because open weaves will allow the wadding to come through. The density of the weave also has a bearing on the weight of a fabric. Heavyweight fabrics are bulky and difficult to manage, so light and medium weights are a better choice. The fibre and weave also determine how much a fabric will fray and those that fray easily make machine piecing and appliqué much more difficult.

Although there are many beautiful fabrics you could choose for your quilt, if you are a beginner, light to medium weight pure cotton is an excellent choice. It has been tried, tested and preferred by quilt makers down the centuries because it washes well, presses pristinely, is easy to stitch and doesn't fray much.

*Polyester and cotton waddings*

*A range of cotton fabrics in closely-related colours*

Whatever your specific preferences, combine fabrics of compatible fibres, weight, construction and care requirements. This will ensure that they are easy to piece together and that when they are joined, you avoid any potential for puckering and one fabric weakening another.

### Tonal value

The colours are probably what draw you to fabrics most, but in fact the tonal value is probably more important to the success of your quilt design. A variety of light, medium and dark tonal values is essential to add depth and vitality. Fabrics of a similar tone merge together so small pieces will appear to flow together to create larger, strong shapes and outlines. Contrasting tones stand out from each other and make the patchwork or appliqué pieces retain their separate identities. So you can create a sense of rhythm in the design by using these principles and the fact that light tones advance and dark ones recede.

You can distinguish the tonal values of different fabrics very easily. Line the fabrics up from light to dark and squint at them – the ones in the wrong position will jump out at you. Or, photocopy small samples together in black and white – the same tones will merge together to look like the same shade of grey and contrasting tones will be obvious.

### Pattern

Although many fabrics are in one solid colour, many others, and especially the pure cottons specifically designed for patchwork, are printed with small, medium or large-scale patterns. Using a combination of different scales of pattern will add visual texture as well as create contrasts that give a sense of movement and maximum impact to the design of a patchwork quilt.

Small-scale patterns look like solid colours from a distance, but instead add interesting detail on closer inspection. Also like solid colours, small patterns tend to be retained within the boundaries of each pieced fabric. In contrast, large-scale patterns look best on larger pieces of fabric and appear to burst out of their boundaries and

*The variation in tone on the half-square triangle border create rhythm on Liberty's Song Bird*

*Variation in scale of patterns on fabric*

flow across the blocks. To help you decide how to position a pattern on patchwork or appliqué pieces, view it through an outline of the template first.

If your design relies on the quilting stitches for its impact, they will show up best on pale, solid colours. So, if you are concerned about uneven stitches on the back of your quilt, choose the safety of a patterned fabric.

### Colour

You will probably have strong ideas about the colours you want to use in your quilt from the outset – perhaps because there are colours you really love and maybe because the quilt has to match an existing colour scheme. You are drawn to different colours because they reflect your own moods or make you feel a particular emotion.

You need more than one colour to make a well-balanced patchwork or appliqué quilt, so it is worth thinking about how you might combine them to create certain moods or effects. The use of certain colours in specific positions will also affect the overall balance of the design and sharp contrasts of colour will have the effect of breaking up quilting lines.

Harmonious colour schemes are created by combining analogous colours – those that are close together on the colour wheel. However, depending on which part of the colour wheel you choose your colours from, you can still achieve very different effects. The cooler nature of greens and blues makes them appear to recede and gives them a peaceful, calming quality often ideal for bedrooms. On the other hand, the hot colours of red and orange tend to advance and dominate – on their own they can be quite overwhelming.

Contrasting colour schemes can be achieved by putting together complementary colours – those that are opposite each other on the colour wheel. Sharp contrasts can be very successful, but you need to be careful with the proportions of your combinations. Equal amounts of red and green will fight each other for attention, whereas a predominantly green scheme, with a little red as an accent, will be stimulating without being overwhelming.

You don't have to use lots of different colours to create exciting designs. Neutral schemes of whites, greys and blacks can look very dramatic. You could also try out a

monochromatic scheme using basically one colour, but with different tonal values to give the design interest.

A good way to decide on the colours for a patchwork or appliqué quilt is to pick one fabric that you absolutely love as the main one. Then select the other fabrics to match secondary colours in the main fabric. You could also choose colour combinations you like by studying the way nature puts colours together, seeing how they are used by other quilt makers from books, magazines and exhibitions, or copying the colours in a favourite photograph. Draw your design on graph paper and colour it in to represent the different colours or consider buying very small quantities to put the fabrics together in roughly the same proportion to see if you still like them together.

Putting together combinations of fabrics, patterns and colours can bring many surprises and be very rewarding. So treat choosing fabric like a great adventure and you're sure to have lots of fun!

*Opposite left: muted earthy and metallic shades combine to give a harmonious effect in Earthspring; opposite top right: a different harmony emerges from the blues and purples in Guardian Angels; opposite bottom right: contrasting colours create a lively effect in the detail of Cocoon*

# Quilt projects

The rich, seductive colours of these silks reminded me of beautiful perfumed roses. So it wasn't long before I was daydreaming about silk roses on a really luxurious quilt. My roses form an extravagant constellation of texture and stitching that reinterpret traditional ideas of quilt design. *Angelina Pieroni*

# Rose constellations

**SIZE**

**Finished quilt:** 160 x 200cm (63 x 79in)

**MATERIALS**

- 140cm-wide (54in-wide) silk:
  - 4.1m (4½yd) in wine red
  - 4.1m (4½yd) in old rose
- 205 x 165cm (81 x 65in) cotton wadding
- Basting thread in a contrasting colour
- Sewing machine thread in toning shades

**Note:** use either metric or imperial measurements; they are not interchangeable

## CUTTING

- Cut 2 strips, measuring 135 x 205cm (53 x 81in) and 32 x 205cm (13 x 81in) from the old rose-coloured silk for the quilt top. Cut 2 strips of the same dimensions from the other silk for the backing.
- Cut enough silk on the bias from the remaining silk to give a total of 5m (5½yd) in each of the following widths: 8cm (3¼in) for the small, 12cm (4½in) for the medium and 15cm (6in) for the large roses.

## LAYERING THE QUILT

1 Piece together the strips for the quilt top, using 1cm (½in) seam. Press the seam to one side. Make the backing in the same way. Lay the backing, right side up, on a flat surface. Smooth the silk for the quilt top, right side down, on top of the backing. Centre the wadding on top. Pin and baste the three layers of the quilt together, making sure that all the edges align.

2 Using a walking foot on the machine and with the wadding on top, sew a 2.5cm (1in) seam around all four edges of the quilt, leaving a 50cm (20in) opening on the bottom edge. Trim the excess fabric at the corners and the wadding along the edges. Press the seams open.

3 Turn the quilt right sides out, carefully coaxing the corners out fully. Pin, baste and slip stitch the open edges together. Then remove the basting stitches and press around the edges of the quilt. Lay the quilt out on a flat surface and safety pin the layers together ready for machine quilting (see page 139).

## MAKING THE ROSES

1 For the small roses, join the short edges of the narrow bias strips together with 6mm (¼in) seams to form one continuous strip of each colour of silk. Press the seams open. Repeat the process with the fabrics for the medium and large roses.

2 Cut the strips for the small roses into 30cm (12in) lengths, those for the medium roses into 50cm (20in) lengths and the ones for the large roses into 70cm (28in) lengths.

3 Fold one of the strips in half lengthways, right sides together. Sew a 6mm (¹⁄₄in) seam around the three raw edges of the strip, leaving a short opening in the long side. Trim the excess fabric at the corners and press the seams open.

4 Turn the strip right sides out, carefully coaxing the corners out fully. Pin, baste and slip stitch the open edges together. Then remove the basting stitches and press around the edges.

5 Securing one end of the thread, sew a gathering thread along the long seamed edge of the strip. Gently pull up the gathering thread so that the strip curls into circles. Wind the strip round to make a rose shape. When you are satisfied with the shape, tuck the end of the strip underneath the rose and fasten off the thread, securing the shape. Squash the rose under your hand, to give it the sharp edges that make it look like a rose rather than a rosette. Practise a few times until you get the right shape.

6 Repeat the same process to make the rest of the roses. The finished roses should be about 10, 8 and 6cm (4, 3¹⁄₄ and 2¹⁄₂in) in diameter. Using thread of a contrasting colour, machine sew two or three lines across each rose, crossing the lines in the centre. Lightly press each rose.

## APPLIQUE AND QUILTING

1 Lay the quilt, right side up, on a flat surface. Put all the roses in a bag and mix them up. Then scatter them randomly onto the quilt. Stand back to decide if you are satisfied with the positioning of the roses. Make any alterations necessary to give an even and pleasing coverage and to create small clusters of different-sized roses. Then pin the roses in position.

2 Using a long ruler and a quilter's pencil, draw lines connecting the roses like stars in constellations. Remember to cross through only the centre of each rose, although some lines can go just into the centre and not come out again on the other side. Extend some lines out to the edge of the quilt, even if there are no roses there. Use the quilt diagram on page 25 as a guide, but you do not have to follow it exactly.

3 Machine sew along the guidelines through all the layers of the quilt to appliqué the roses into position. Make sure that each rose is attached to the quilt with at least two crossing lines. Where the occasional line of stitches ends without a rose, sew three more lines across the end to make small thread stars (see the illustration left). Remove the safety pins as you stitch the layers together. Fasten off and trim any loose quilting threads.

## QUILT CARE

This quilt could be either hand washed or dry-cleaned, although you might prefer to sponge it with a damp cloth to remove small stains to avoid excessive cleaning.

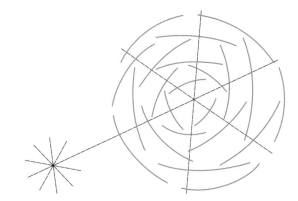

*Stitching across a silk rose and making a stitched star*

## ADAPTING THIS DESIGN

The very nature of this design encourages you to be creative. You can scatter the roses completely randomly or place them in a particular pattern. Just remember to stitch into all the corners so that the layers are quilted together across the whole quilt.

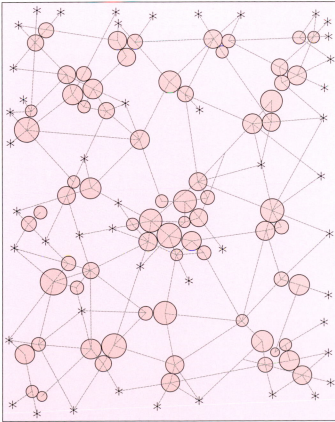

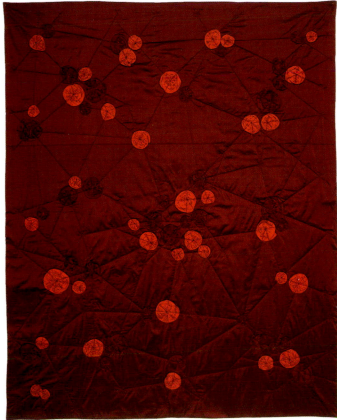

I designed this quilt in a very spontaneous way, moving fabrics around on the floor in the same way that the abstract painters who inspire me might lay down one surprising block of colour next to another. Lime green, purple and white sound rather wild together, but when I saw them in the different textures of silk, linen and velvet, the whole design started to develop a pleasing balance. *Karen Spurgin*

# Art Deco abstract

**SIZE**

Finished quilt: 150 x 200cm (60 x 80in)

**MATERIALS**

- 112cm-wide (44in-wide) fabrics:
  - 1.55m (1³⁄₄yd) velvet in purple
  - 50cm (20in) linen in lilac
  - 50cm (20in) silk in lime
  - 50cm (20in) striped silk
  - 50cm (20in) silk in lilac
  - 50cm (20in) silk dupion in white
  - 30cm (12in) velvet in white
  - 10cm (4in) organza in silver
- 4.2m x 90cm-wide (4¹⁄₂yd x 36in-wide) cotton fabric in lilac (backing)
- 202 x 152cm (81 x 61in) lightweight polyester wadding
- Sewing machine thread in toning colours
- Basting thread in a contrasting colour

**Note:** use either metric or imperial measurements; they are not interchangeable

*Quilter's tip: If you find it hard to visualize the overall effect, make a collage of the design using tiny pieces of the actual fabrics.*

## DESIGNING YOUR QUILT

The beauty of this quilt is that it can be made in different combinations and proportions of fabric. The interplay of different textures was a key inspiration, resulting in broad swathes of deep velvet next to exotic silk and shimmering silver organza laid over some of the small white silk pieces.

You might like to draw the diagram on page 29 to scale on graph paper, so that you can plan the positions of your fabrics with coloured pencils. Alternatively, you could start with a blank rectangle and decide for yourself on the depths of the strips that go across the quilt. If you keep your sketch to scale, you will be able to cut the fabrics to the correct sizes very easily – remembering the seam allowances all round of course.

## CUTTING

- Cut the velvet along its length into 3 strips of the depths given on the diagram, adding 1cm (¹⁄₂in) seam allowances all round. The extra-wide seam allowance is recommended because the velvets and silks have a great tendency to fray very easily.
- Cut enough fabric to piece together the other one-fabric strips that go across the quilt, following the depths given on the diagram and adding 1cm (¹⁄₂in) seam allowances all round.
- For the two multi-fabric strips, cut the remaining linen, silk and velvet into 7cm (3in) strips.
- Cut the backing fabric into two lengths, but do not trim it to size at this stage.

## PIECING THE STRIPS

1 First make the two multi-fabric strips. Choose the order of the fabrics as you go or follow your design diagram. Pin and baste the first two fabrics, aligning the short edges right sides together. Sew them together with a 2cm (¹⁄₂in) seam.

Remove the basting stitches and press the seam towards the darker fabric, taking special precautions if you are pressing the velvet (see page 117). Decide how wide you would like each piece of fabric to be and cut the pieces accordingly.

2 Now choose the third fabric and sew it to the strip in the same way. Trim it to the appropriate width. Keep adding fabrics to the strip until it is 152cm (61in) long. Then make the second strip in the same way.

3 Pin, baste and sew together the pieces to make each of the one-fabric strips. Remove the basting threads and press the seams to one side.

4 Pin and baste the top two strips, right sides together, along their lengths. Sew the strips together with a 1cm (½in) seam. Remove the basting stitches and press the seam to one side. Piece the rest of the strips together in the same way.

### LAYERING THE QUILT

1 Check that the corners of the quilt top are square and the sides are straight. Piece the fabric for the backing together in the usual way using a 6mm (¼in) seam (see page 137). Press the seams to opposite sides.

2 Lay the backing, right side up, on a flat surface. Centre the quilt top, right side down, on the backing. Pin and baste them together. Then trim the backing to the same size as the quilt top. Lay the wadding over the quilt top. Pin and baste the three layers together and trim the wadding to the same size.

3 Using a walking foot and with the wadding on top, machine sew a 1cm (½in) seam around all four edges of the quilt, leaving a 50cm (20in) opening on the bottom edge. Trim the excess fabric at the corners and remove all the remaining basting stitches.

4 Turn the quilt right sides out, coaxing the corners out fully. Press the edges of the quilt. Pin, baste and slip stitch (see page 112) the opening together. Remove the basting stitches.

### QUILTING

Baste the layers of the quilt together in the usual way (see page 138). Using thread in toning colours, quilt in the ditch (see page 136) along the horizontal seam lines. Remove all the basting stitches and shake out the quilt to fluff it up.

### QUILT CARE

Because this quilt combines very different fabrics, it is not suitable for washing. Instead, take it to a reputable dry-cleaner.

### ADAPTING THIS DESIGN

Patchwork has always been a way of recycling fabric. Use the fabric from your favourite clothes when they no longer fit and other scraps of fabric to make a very personal interpretation of this quilt.

## KEY TO QUILT DIAGRAM

**A** = purple velvet

**B** = lilac linen

**C** = lime silk

**D** = striped silk

**E** = lilac silk

**F** = white silk dupion

**G** = white velvet

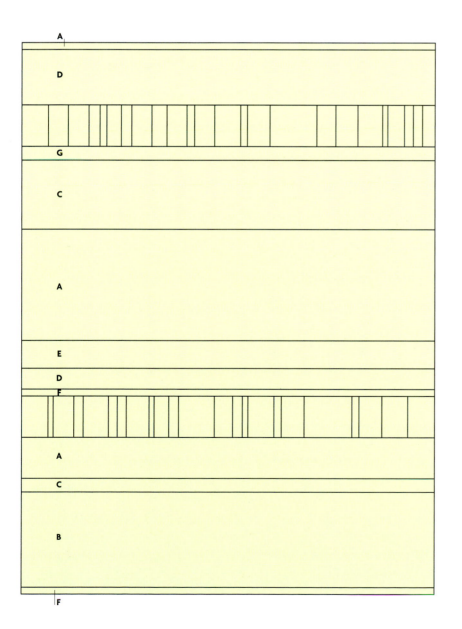

This deceptively simple quilt is the epitome of cool elegance. It marries together echoes of two very sophisticated cultures — the cream on navy is reminiscent of Japanese Sashiko, while the toile de Jouy-like print — and not least the knots — are very French. The simple construction makes a cosy quilt that would keep away the chills of a winter's evening, but could just as well provide a comfy place to sit in a summer garden. *Karen Spurgin*

# French knots on navy

**SIZE**
Finished quilt: 95 x 190cm (37$\frac{1}{2}$ x 74$\frac{3}{4}$in)

**MATERIALS**
- 112cm-wide (44in-wide) fabrics:
  - 2m (2$\frac{1}{4}$yd) linen in navy
  - 2m (2$\frac{1}{4}$yd) lightweight cotton (lining)
  - 2m (2$\frac{1}{4}$yd) floral cotton (backing)
- 100 x 195cm (40 x 77in) medium-weight polyester wadding
- 4 balls coton perlé No 5 in white
- Sewing machine thread in a toning colour
- Basting thread in a contrasting colour

**Note:** use either metric or imperial measurements; they are not interchangeable

## CUTTING

- Cut the linen, cotton lining and backing fabric to 100 x 195cm (40 x 77in).

## QUILTING

1 First ensure that the edges of the linen are absolutely square. Then fold it in half lengthways to find the midpoints on the top and bottom edges. Mark the midpoints with pins. Repeat the process to find the midpoints on the side edges.

2 Smooth the linen out, right side up, on a flat surface. Using a long ruler and a quilter's pencil, join up the two sets of pins so that you have two very faint lines crossing in the middle of the fabric. Mark the centre of the fabric with a dot. Then mark dots along each line at 5cm (2in) intervals. Working out from the centre lines, very accurately mark a grid of dots on the fabric at 5cm (2in) intervals. Each dot marks the position for a French knot.

3 Lay the wadding on a flat surface and centre the lining fabric on top. The lining prevents the fibres of the wadding from being pulled through the linen when the French knots are made. Finally, centre the linen quilt top, right side up, on top of the lining. Pin or baste the layers together in the usual way (see pages 138–9).

4 Work the French knots in rows across the quilt. Using a large crewel needle, secure a double length of the coton perlé, no more than 50cm (20in) long, in the lining fabric. Bring the needle up through the first marked dot and make a French knot, twisting the thread round the needle three times (see page 112). Secure the knot with a back stitch and take the needle down through the layers. Bring the needle back up through the next dot to make the second French knot on the same line. Continue making knots along this and then successive lines until the whole grid is complete.

## FINISHING THE QUILT

1 Smooth the floral backing fabric, right side up, on a flat surface. Centre the quilt, right side down, on top. Pin and baste the layers together, making sure that the edges align.

2 Machine sew a 2.5cm (1in) seam around all the edges of the quilt, leaving a 50cm (20in) opening on the bottom edge. Trim the excess fabric at the corners and then trim the seam allowances back to 6mm (¼in). Press the seams open.

3 Turn the quilt right sides out, carefully coaxing the corners out fully. Pin, baste and slip stitch the open edges together. Then remove the basting stitches and press around the edges of the quilt.

4 Lay the quilt on a flat surface and baste the edges. Using coton perlé, work two lines of stab stitch (see page 111) round all the edges.

5 Remove any loose threads or lint. Using a pressing cloth to prevent getting a shine on the linen, very lightly steam-press the quilt.

## QUILT CARE

This quilt is suitable for machine washing on a gentle cycle and drying on a washing line.

## ADAPTING THIS DESIGN

■ Hand tie the quilt (see page 141), instead of using French knots.
■ Choose bold fabric colours and a contrasting thread for the stitches to make a loud, fun statement.
■ Try using a satin fabric and a lightweight wadding to make a soft, sexy wrap.

Part of the joy of this quilt is rummaging around in antique markets and taking your pick in specialist shops to find the ribbons, new and old. I collected together all sorts of different ones in the colours of a calm sea to make a quilt that would soothe anyone to sleep. Your own choice of ribbons will give the quilt a very personal character. *Karen Spurgin*

# Sea of dreams

**SIZE**

Finished quilt: 100 x 150cm (40 x 60in)

Finished block (15): 25 x 25cm (10 x 10in)

**MATERIALS**

■ 90 x 150cm (36 x 60in) lightweight cotton (blocks)

■ 50m (55yds) assorted ribbons in blues, greens and lilacs

■ Madeira Décor thread in white

■ Natesh Empress thread in shade 64

■ Natesh Titania thread in shade 101L

■ 1.6m x 140cm-wide (2yds x 54in-wide) patterned fabric in pale blue (borders)

■ 80 x 140cm-wide (32 x 54in-wide) patterned cotton in pale blue (backing)

■ 80 x 130cm (32 x 52in) wadding

■ Sewing machine threads in toning colours

■ Basting thread in contrasting colours

**Note:** use either metric or imperial measurements; they are not interchangeable

## SELECTING THE RIBBONS

Choose a wide range of ribbons from 4mm to 10cm ($^3/_{16}$–4in) wide. They could include new and old ribbons, different materials such as silk, transparent organza and metallic threads, and different textures from shiny satin to grosgrain.

## CUTTING

■ 15 squares, each 30 x 30cm (12 x 12in), in the fabric for the blocks.

■ Cut the ribbons into 30cm (12in) lengths.

■ 2 strips, each 31 x 155cm (12$^1/_2$ x 65in), in the border fabric (side borders).

■ 2 strips, each 31 x 105cm (12$^1/_2$ x 45in), in the border fabric (top and bottom borders).

■ Do not cut the wadding or backing until the blocks have been pieced together.

## PIECING THE BLOCKS

1 Lay the squares of cotton fabric for the blocks in five rows of three on a flat surface. It helps to work on all the blocks at the same time to ensure that they complement each other well.

2 Cover each block with the lengths of ribbon. Align some ribbons selvedge to selvedge, but allow others to overlap. Add accents to wide ribbons by placing very narrow ribbons on top. Mix the different textures and experiment with layering the transparent organza ribbons. Imagine you are creating an abstract painting. Pin all the ribbons in place and then stand back to check that you are satisfied with the whole composition. Then baste the ribbons to secure them in place.

3 Begin to stitch down the edges of the ribbons using either running stitch or herringbone stitch (see pages 110 and 113). Not only will these stitches secure the ribbons to the blocks, they will also add decorative detail to the quilt. Use the

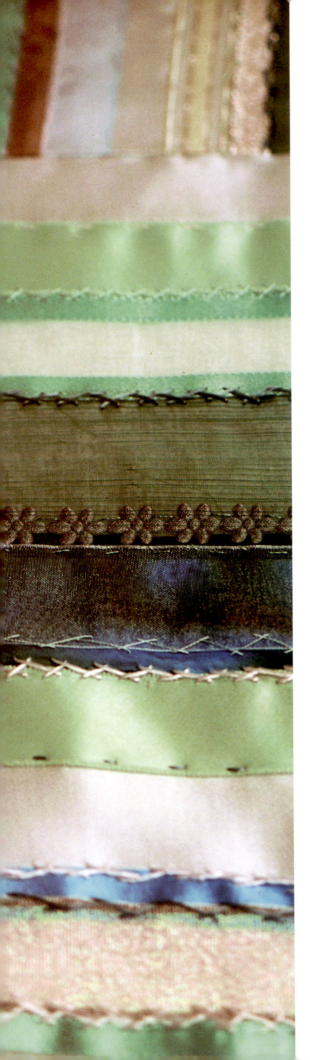

two stitches and the three embroidery threads in a random order. Try out lots of different variations, such as a row of herringbone stitch in the thick thread right next to another row of herringbone in the fine thread, or a tiny running stitch followed by a wide herringbone stitch. It's these variations that will add to the depth and beauty of the quilt.

4 Remove all the basting stitches and, using a pressing cloth, press the blocks. Pin and baste each row of three blocks together with 2.5cm (1in) seams. The extra allowance in the seams is recommended to allow the ribbon ends to lie flat. Then machine stitch the blocks together to make up the rows. Remove the basting stitches and press all the seams to one side.

5 Pin and baste the five rows together, with 2.5cm (1in) seams. Then machine stitch them together to complete the quilt top. Remove the basting stitches and press all the seams as before.

## QUILTING

1 Check that the corners of the quilt top are square and the sides are straight. Trim the quilt top as necessary. Layer and baste the backing, wadding and quilt top in the usual way for quilting by hand (see pages 138–9).

2 Quilt in the ditch (see page 136) along the seams between the blocks with stab stitch (see page 111). Remove all the basting stitches and fasten off any loose quilting threads. Trim the wadding and backing to the same size as the quilt top.

## FINISHING THE QUILT

1 To make the borders, press the four strips of fabric in half lengthways. Then press a 2.5cm (1in) turning to the wrong side of the fabric along one long edge of each of the strips.

2 Find the midpoints along the sides of the quilt top and the borders. Align the long, raw edge of each border to the corresponding edge of the quilt top, matching up the midpoints. Machine sew first the side borders and then the top and bottom borders in place with a 2.5cm (1in) seam. Sew exactly to the points on the corners where the borders meet, but no further. Press the seam allowances towards the borders.

3 To mitre a corner, first mark out the mitre seam line on the wrong side of the fabric. Lay the quilt top, right side down, on a flat surface with the side border smoothed out underneath the adjoining border. Open out the turning allowance too and put a pin through the point where the two pairs of folded edges cross. Using a water-erasable marker or a quilter's pencil, mark the mitre line from the inner corner of the border to the centre fold line. Then mark another line at right angles to the first from the point where one pair of folded edges cross to the point where the second pair cross. (See the illustration on page 37.) Then switch the two borders round, so that the side border lies on top of the other one. Repeat the process to give two lines to correspond with the first two.

4 Align the v-shaped seam on both borders. Machine along the seam, starting very precisely at the corner where the quilt layers meet the borders, pivoting on the point of the v and stopping where the two turning folds on the borders meet. Trim the excess fabric close across the point of the v and to 6mm (¼in) along the seams. Press the seams open and turn the corner of the border out. Repeat the process to mitre the remaining three corners.

5 Fold the turning allowance on the raw edges of the borders to the wrong side again. Pin each border to hold the folded edges in place. Then pin and baste the borders into position around the wrong side of the quilt top. Slip stitch the edges in place and remove the basting stitches. When you have finished, shake the quilt out to fluff it up.

## QUILT CARE

Because the ribbons are made of various fibres, the quilt is not suitable for washing. Instead, take it to a reputable dry-cleaner.

## ADAPTING THIS DESIGN

■ Use the ribbons from your children's clothes after they have grown out of them to make a quilt that can be passed down to your grandchildren.

■ Save the ribbon from Christmas and birthday present wrappings to make a quilt full of happy memories.

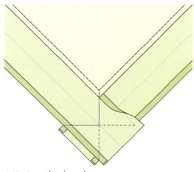

*Mitring the borders*

I love to work with Welsh woollen cloths and the cosy warmth they give to this quilt is very satisfying. The result is a design that has a rustic charm, with an element of fun from the bright little pompoms. It's perfect to curl up in! *Hikaru Noguchi*

# Pompom maze

**SIZE**
Finished quilt: 110 x 220cm (45 x 90in)
**MATERIALS**
- 140cm-wide (54in-wide) wool flannel:
  - 50cm (20in) in white
  - 50cm (20in) in beige
  - 50cm (20in) in orange stripe
  - 50cm (20in) in grey stripe
  - 2.1m (2⅓yd) in navy
- 2.2m x 112cm-wide (2½yd x 44in-wide) cotton print (backing)
- 110 x 220cm (45 x 90in) wadding of your choice
- Basting thread in a contrasting colour
- Sewing machine thread in a complementary colour
- Knitting wool in complementary colours (pompoms)

**Note:** use either metric or imperial measurements; they are not interchangeable

## CUTTING

- 48 squares, 10 x 10 cm (4 x 4in), from each of the five woollen fabrics (centre panel).
- 2 strips, 17 x 224cm (6 ¾ x 91in), from the navy flannel (side borders).
- 2 strips, 17 x 112cm (6 ¾ x 46in), from the navy flannel (top and bottom borders).

## PIECING THE QUILT TOP

1 Start by piecing together the top row of shapes for the centre panel, following the quilt diagram on page 41. Pin, baste and machine sew the shapes wrong sides together, using a 1cm (⅜in) seam allowance. Then piece together each of the other rows in the same way. Remove the basting threads and press all the seams open. Now join the rows together in the same way, following the diagram.

2 Smooth the centre panel, right side up, on a flat surface. The right side displays all the seam allowances, which are a particular feature of this design. Check that the edges are straight and the corners are square, and trim the panel as necessary. Put a pin at the midpoint along each edge and measure across the middle of the quilt from pin to opposite pin to give you more precise measurements for the side, top and bottom borders. Add seam allowances of 1cm (⅜in) all round to these measurements.

3 Mark the midpoint along one long edge of each border. Place one of the side borders, right side down, along one long side of the centre panel and pin the midpoints together. Pin the ends of the border in place and then, aligning the edges, pin the rest of the seam. Baste the seam, easing the edges to fit. Sew the border in place with a 1cm (⅜in) seam, starting and stopping exactly 1cm (⅜in) away from the adjacent edge. Attach the other three borders in the same way. Remove the basting stitches and press the seam allowances towards the borders.

4 Mitre the corners of the borders, working on the wrong side of the fabric and following the instructions on pages 126–7. Machine sew the mitred seams

together. Trim the seam allowances. Remove any remaining basting stitches and press the seams open.

## LAYERING THE QUILT

1 Again, make sure that the edges of the quilt top are straight and the corners are square. Trim the quilt top as necessary. Lay the backing, right side up, on a flat surface. Centre the quilt top, right side down, on the backing. Centre the wadding over the quilt top. Pin and baste all three layers together. Then trim the backing and wadding to the same size as the quilt top.

2 Using a walking foot and with the wadding on top, machine sew a 1cm (³⁄₈in) seam around all four edges of the quilt, leaving a 50cm (20in) opening on the bottom edge. Trim the seam allowance and the excess fabric at the corners. Remove all the basting stitches. Turn the quilt right sides out, coaxing the corners out fully.

3 Press the open edges of the quilt. Pin, baste and slip stitch (see page 112) the opening together. Remove the basting stitches.

## FINISHING THE QUILT

1 Safety pin the layers of the quilt together in the usual way (see pages 138–9). Machine sew a running stitch 1cm (³⁄₈in) in from all the edges. Machine quilt in the ditch (see page 136) along the border seams.

2 Make as many pompoms as you wish to embellish the quilt top, randomly choosing the colours of yarn to match the fabrics. Cut a rectangular piece of card with the shorter sides the same measurement as the radius of the finished pompom, plus an extra 1.5cm (⁵⁄₈in). Cut a tying thread about 20cm (8in) long and lay this along one of the long edges of the card. Wrap the chosen yarn generously around the card and the tying thread until the pompom has the appropriate bulk. Tie the ends of the tying thread tightly around the wrapped threads with a double knot. Cut through the wrapped loops at the opposite end to the tying thread. Shake the pompom vigorously to fluff it out. Then trim the lengths of yarn to shape a sphere. (This method is similar to the one for making tassels on page 76.)

3 Use the tying threads to attach the pompoms to the quilt, sewing them through all the layers and fastening them off on the backing side.

## QUILT CARE

If you make this quilt of woollen cloth, it is not recommended for washing. Instead, take it to a reputable dry-cleaner.

## ADAPTING THIS DESIGN

■ For a more refined effect, turn the seam allowances to the wrong side of the centre panel.

■ Try using a heavier weight of wadding and hand tie the layers of the quilt together.

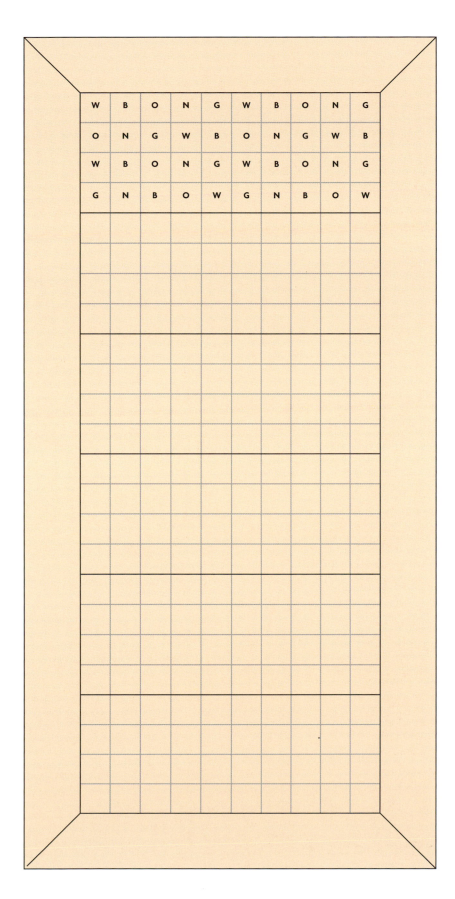

| W | B | O | N | G | W | B | O | N | G |
| O | N | G | W | B | O | N | G | W | B |
| W | B | O | N | G | W | B | O | N | G |
| G | N | B | O | W | G | N | B | O | W |

## KEY TO QUILT DIAGRAM

**W** = white

**B** = beige

**O** = orange stripe

**G** = grey stripe

**N** = navy

It was the plush textures and embroidery on Victorian crazy patchwork that inspired me to begin quilting, and I still prefer working with velvets and other luxury fabrics. Each of these evening fabrics is glamorous, taking on a new, seductive life in different lights. I could see them on an olive background, so finding a taffeta that was wide enough to make a large quilt was a real bonus. *Esther MacFarlane*

# Bejewelled seams

## CUTTING

- 1 piece, 145 x 205cm (57 x 81in), in olive green taffeta (centre panel, including the top and bottom borders).
- 2 strips, both 32 x 205cm (12 x 81in) in olive green taffeta (side borders). If the fabric has a nap, make sure that the nap runs down the length of the side borders in the same direction as it does down the centre panel. Retain the remaining taffeta to make the binding later.
- 2 strips, 210cm (83in) long in sateen cotton (backing). The width of the backing will be trimmed later.
- Cut all the fabrics for the blocks in half lengthways to give two 30cm (12in) strips from each fabric. This allows you to add interest by using the fabric grain in either the same or different directions. Leave the velvet to one side and cut the silk strips into 30cm (12in) squares.
- Retain the rest of the block fabrics and the taffeta to make the binding later. Do not trim the wadding at this stage.

## PIECING THE BLOCKS

All the blocks are cut freehand with a rotary cutter and it is a good idea to practise this technique on some spare fabric until you feel confident. This technique produces seams in the same direction, which take up fabric. The blocks are then trimmed into squares.

1 Place one square of fabric on the cutting mat and put another one, both right sides up and perfectly aligned, on top. Work with the fabric colours in any order – the variety will add richness to the finished blocks. In Bejewelled Seams, the black viscose velvet has no nap and provides a dense foil for the colours, viewed from every direction.

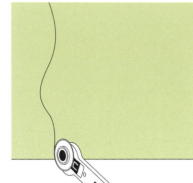

*Cutting a gently curving line across the first two fabrics*

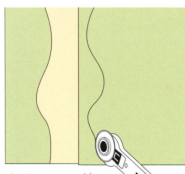

*Cutting a curved line across the next pair of fabrics*

2 Using the rotary cutter and starting from one edge, cut a gently curving line from the top to the bottom edges of both layers of fabric. The resulting curved strip should be between 4–8cm (1½–3¼in) wide.

3 Separate the fabrics and pair up one piece of the top fabric with the complementary piece of the bottom fabric. Pair the other two pieces together. When you lay each pair together, right sides up, the cut lines should fit snugly.

4 With a quilter's pencil, mark a few registration marks along the curved edges inside the 6mm (¼in) seam allowances on the wrong side of the neighbouring pieces of fabric. The more curved the line, the more marks you will need to help you match the seams.

5 Pick up a pair of the cut fabrics, leaving the other pair safely to one side. Place the two pieces right sides together and pin them through the registration marks. If necessary, clip into the seam allowance along the curves to allow them to ease into place (see pages 124–5). Pin the rest of the seam together. Sew a 6mm (¼in) seam, removing the pins as you go. Press the seams towards the darker fabric. Take care when pressing the velvet and follow the advice on page 117. Repeat the process on the other pair of fabrics.

6 Lay one of the pieced fabrics on the cutting mat and put a third fabric on top of it, both right sides up. Align the top and bottom edges of the fabrics, but offset the side edges so that the next cut line will make an attractive curved strip on the bottom fabric (see left). Cut another curving line through both layers with the rotary cutter. Separate the layers and swop the pairs over as before. Piece both pairs of fabrics together and press the seams.

7 Continue piecing curved strips together in the same way until you have a total of nine blocks, each measuring at least 30cm (12in) square. Place each block on the cutting mat and carefully trim it to 30cm (12in) square, which includes the further seam allowances.

### PIECING THE QUILT

1 Lay the largest piece of background fabric right side up on a flat surface. Measure 31cm (12¼in) in from each end along each long side of the fabric and mark with pins. Mark two lines 31cm (12¼in) in from the top and bottom across the width of the fabric between the two sets of pins. The strips at the top and the bottom form part of the border of the quilt.

2 Pin a turning of 1cm (½in) under around all the edges on each block. Baste the turnings in place. Place the blocks, right side up, spacing them at equal intervals across the central square panel of the background fabric. Arrange the blocks in the most pleasing order, alternating the direction of the strips. When you are happy with the visual balance, pin the blocks to the background fabric.

3 Stretch the quilt in a hoop, so that you can work on one block. First baste the block in position and then hand stitch it to the background fabric with either running (see page 110) or slip stitch (see page 112). Release the fabric from the hoop and remove the basting stitches. Repeat the process on the other eight blocks.

4 Aligning the long edges right sides together, pin the two side borders along each of the two long edges of the main background piece. Sew the borders in place with 6mm (¼in) seams. Press both seams towards the borders.

## QUILTING

1 Piece the fabric for the backing together in the usual way, using a 6mm (¼in) seam (see pages 137–8). Trim the backing so that it is 5cm (2in) bigger than the quilt top all round. Cut the wadding so that it is slightly smaller than the backing. Layer the backing, wadding and quilt top (see page 138). Safety pin the layers together in a grid pattern so that you avoid stitching across the blocks (see page 139).

2 A fairly long stitch and a No 9 needle suited the taffeta, but experiment to find the right combination for your fabric. Machine quilt in the ditch (see page 136) around the centre panel, along the side seams and across the guidelines at the top and bottom. Remove the safety pins as you go.

3 Start quilting between the blocks in the centre panel. Begin on the edge of the panel, close to one of the blocks, and stitch a gently curving line to the opposite side of the centre panel. Return to where you started and sew another curved line a short distance away. Continue in the same way until you have worked right round the square so that the quilting crosses at the intersections. Quilt along each of the borders in the same way so that the quilting crosses at the outer corners.

## FINISHING THE QUILT

1 Fasten off any loose quilting threads. Trim the backing and wadding to the same size as the quilt top. Check that the corners are square and the sides are straight.

2 Cut 6cm (2½in) strips from the taffeta and all the fabrics used in the blocks ready to make a mitred border (see pages 126–7). Stitch the strips together with 6mm (¼in) seams, deciding on the order of the colours and the length of each piece as you go. Make four lengths, one for each side of the quilt, remembering to allow extra for mitring the corners and seams.

3 Attach the strips to the quilt to make a mitred binding in the usual way, allowing a 6mm (¼in) seam on the binding and a 2cm (¾in) seam on the quilt. The extra seam allowance on the quilt pads out the binding, adding to the luxurious quality of the quilt. When you have finished, shake out the quilt to fluff it up.

## QUILT CARE

This quilt is not suitable for washing. Instead, take it to a reputable dry-cleaner. Oily products will make an obvious stain on taffeta. Should that happen, sprinkle talcum powder over the stain, leave it to soak up the oil and then brush it off.

## ADAPTING THIS DESIGN

■ Make the quilt in cotton fabrics so that it can be washed.

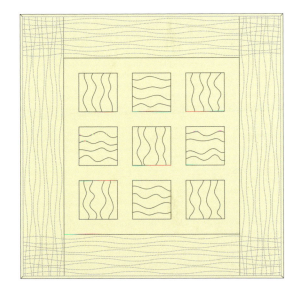

We all wish for the very best for our children, so in my imagination this quilt represents a snug cocoon of peace and harmony. As flowers of harmony float down from the sky, the little bird sings a song of peace that will lull any baby to sleep.

*Hiroko Aono-Billson*

# Liberty's song bird

## SIZE

**Finished quilt:** 100 x 120cm (40 x 48in)

**Finished border block (40):** 10 x 10cm (4 x 4in)

## MATERIALS

■ Selection of cotton prints to make 40 blocks and the appliqué shapes, plus seam allowances

■ 1.25m x 90cm-wide (1¼yd x 36in-wide) cotton in cream (background and posts)

■ 1.3m x 112cm-wide (1½yd x 44in-wide) brushed cotton in cream (backing)

■ 35cm x 112cm-wide (14 x 44in-wide) cotton print (binding)

■ 110 x 130cm (44 x 52in) cotton wadding

■ Quilting thread in cream and red

■ Sewing machine thread in cream

■ Stranded cotton embroidery threads in peppermint green, and pale and dark pink

■ Basting thread in a contrasting colour

■ 9 small and 6 large wool pompoms in red

**Note:** use either metric or imperial measurements; they are not interchangeable

## PIECING THE CENTRE PANEL

1 Tape together pieces of card or paper to make one 90 x 110cm (36 x 43in) sheet to use for the pattern. Using the grid method on page 128, enlarge the design on page 149 onto the prepared sheet so that the outline measures 80 x 100cm (32 x 40in). Transfer all the labels and instructions on the design outline to your pattern. Lay the pattern out on a flat surface and trace each shape onto tracing or greaseproof (waxed) paper. Label each template as on the pattern. Cut out all the templates.

2 Referring to the photograph of the quilt on page 49, determine which shapes you want to cut from each of your fabrics. Lay the fabrics out, right side down, on a flat surface. Flip each of the templates over, right side down, onto the wrong side of the relevant fabric. Pin each one to the fabric, leaving enough space for a 6mm (¼in) turning allowance around each shape. Cut all the shapes out of the fabric, adding the turning allowance to each one. Press and baste the turnings under on each of the shapes. You may find that it helps to clip into the seam allowance around the shapes for the bird's body and wing.

3 Cut a piece of the cream background cotton measuring 80 x 100cm (32 x 40in), plus seam allowances, for the centre panel. If you wish, trace the pattern onto the right side of the fabric, using a pastel quilter's pencil (see page 129). Alternatively, keep the pattern to use as a guide for positioning the appliqué.

4 Lay the centre panel, right side up, on a flat surface. Pin and baste the appliqué shapes in position. Take care to position the ends of the small branches under the large branch, the flower petals over the ends of the stems and the bird's wing on top of its body. Using cream thread, slip stitch (see page 112) the appliqué shapes in position. Remove the basting stitches and lightly press the panel on the wrong side.

5 Using three strands of the green cotton embroidery thread, work a double row of back stitch (see page 111) for each of the feathers on the bird's head and tail. Then attach a large pompom to the end of each feather.

6 Work a double row of back stitch for the bird's legs, this time using three strands of the dark pink cotton embroidery thread. Then using six strands of the same dark pink thread, embroider the bird's eye with a double row of back stitch.

7 Complete the embroidery on the centre panel by stitching the flower stamen in three strands of pale pink and the veins of the leaves in three strands of green cotton embroidery thread. Attach one small pompom on the end of each of the flower stamens.

## PIECING THE BORDERS

Cut the fabrics for the border as follows:

- four squares, each 11.2 x 11.2cm (4$\frac{1}{2}$ x 4$\frac{1}{2}$in), from the cream cotton (corner posts).
- 16 squares of different cotton prints, each 12.1 x 12.1cm (4$\frac{7}{8}$ x 4$\frac{7}{8}$in); then cut each square in half diagonally to make 32 half-square triangles (see page 122).
- 20 squares of different cotton prints, each 13 x 13cm (11$\frac{1}{4}$ x 11$\frac{1}{4}$in); cut each square in half diagonally and then each triangle in half to make 80 quarter-square triangles (see page 122).

1 Chain piece (see page 125) pairs of quarter-square triangles together, using a 6mm ($\frac{1}{4}$in) seam allowance, to make bigger triangles. Separate the triangles and press the seams towards the darker fabrics. Then piece together these new triangles in the same way to make 20 squares – 10 squares for each of the side borders – and press the seams to one side.

2 Chain piece pairs of half-square triangles together, using a 6mm ($\frac{1}{4}$in) seam allowance, to make 16 squares – 8 of the squares for each of the top and bottom borders – adding a plain cream corner post to each end of each border. Press the seams to one side.

## COMPLETING THE QUILT TOP

1 Mark the midpoints on each side of the centre panel and also the midpoint on one long edge of each of the borders. Pin and baste each of the side borders to the centre panel, matching the markings right sides together. Using 6mm ($\frac{1}{4}$in) seam allowances, machine sew the borders in place. Remove the basting stitches and press the seams towards the borders.

2 Attach the top and bottom borders in the same way, matching midpoint markings and the seams joining the pieced blocks to the centre panel and corner posts.

3 Trace the flower design for the corner posts from the pattern on page 148. Place the tracing over a light source and, using a pastel quilter's pencil, transfer the design outline to the right side of each square of fabric for the corner posts (see page 129), ready to quilt them later. Make sure each flower opens out towards the outer corner.

## QUILTING

1 Fasten off any loose threads on the quilt top. Layer and baste the backing, wadding and quilt top together in the usual way (see pages 138–9).

2 Using cream thread and stitching by hand, outline quilt 3mm (⅛in) outside the edge of each appliquéd shape. Still using the cream thread and referring to the diagram for the spacing, stitch a diagonal grid of star stitch (see page 113) across the cream background of the centre panel.

3 Using cream thread, quilt in the ditch (see page 136) around the centre panel. Quilt in the same way inside the edges of the top and bottom triangles in each of the side border blocks. Then quilt a diagonal line from top left to bottom right across each of the blocks in the top and bottom borders.

4 Finally, using the red quilting thread, quilt around the outlines of the flowers on each corner post. Work a French knot (see page 112) on the end of each stamen with two strands of pale pink cotton embroidery thread.

## FINISHING THE QUILT

1 Check that the corners of the quilt are square and the sides are straight. Trim the quilt as necessary.

2 Take measurements across the midpoints of the quilt and calculate how long the strip of binding needs to be, adding an additional 50cm (20in). Cut enough 6.5cm (2½in) strips of fabric on the straight or cross grain to make the binding. Following the instructions on pages 143–4, attach a double binding to the quilt.

## QUILT CARE

If you make this quilt in cotton fabrics and you know that the pompoms are colour fast, it can be washed by hand in lukewarm water. Gently squeeze the excess water from the quilt and dry it flat, in the shade, outdoors. Tease the pompoms back into shape when dry.

## ADAPTING THIS DESIGN

Try a different colour scheme to suit the personality of the child lucky enough to receive the quilt.

This very rich scrap quilt is my personal celebration of the multiculturalism of Australia. I used fabrics from many different cultures and countries, but chose the motif of eucalyptus leaves to unify the design and symbolize Australia. The hand-dyed fabrics forming the background are cut through in the technique of reverse appliqué to reveal the opulent colours, threads and textures of the leaves. *Jan Clark*

# Gumleaves

## SELECTING THE FABRICS

You could use all kinds of fabrics for this design. On Gumleaves, the leaf fabrics include Chinese brocades, Indian silks, African Jacquards, Balinese batiks, glitz from evening wear, sequins and lace, as well as printed cottons from many countries. For the background fabrics, choose ones that blend well together – they might be closely related colours, like different purples, or colours of the same value, such as pastels. This will make the leaves stand out, especially if the fabrics for each block contrast well with each other.

## CUTTING

■ 100 rectangles, each 11.2 x 16.2cm (4½ x 6½in), for the leaves.
■ 100 rectangles, each 11.2 x 16.2cm (4½ x 6½in), for the backgrounds.
■ 5 strips, each 6.5cm (2½in) wide and cut across the fabric width, for the binding.
■ Do not the cut the backing or wadding to size until the quilt top has been finished.

## PIECING THE BLOCKS

1 Using a permanent black marker, trace the design of the three leaves in the rectangle on page 146 onto a sheet of paper. With the aid of a light box and a quilter's pencil, mark the leaf outlines on the right side of each of the background rectangles. The shapes are very simple and after you have sewn them a few times you may prefer not to mark the fabric at all, but simply sew three leaves without marking them first.

2 Place a piece of background fabric on top of a contrasting leaf fabric, both right sides up. Pin them together. Set the machine stitch length to 2 or 3. Using a running stitch, machine sew twice around the outline of each leaf shape. You will need to pivot the fabric around the needle at the point of each leaf, but do not need to follow the exact line of the design. Fasten off and cut the threads.

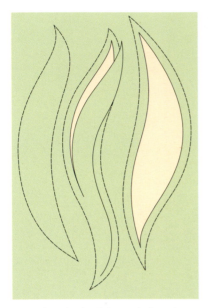

*Revealing the leaf shapes below the top fabric*

3 Pull the two fabrics apart inside one of the design outlines and, using sharp, pointed scissors, snip into the top fabric. Carefully cut out the leaf shape inside the design outline. Then cut out the other two leaves, to reveal the leaf fabric beneath the background.

4 Make all the blocks in the same way. Then lightly iron them and trim each one to the same size. Arrange the blocks on the floor or a similar flat surface, either referring to the photograph on page 53 or piecing them together in your own way to make up the rectangular quilt top. Swap blocks around until you are happy with the overall balance of the design.

5 Draw a quick sketch of your design and label each block on the sketch. Then put the correct label on the back of each corresponding fabric block. Look at your sketch again and decide on the bigger sections that you can piece together to minimise and simplify the seams you need to sew. Note this order of working on your sketch.

6 Machine sew all the blocks together to make bigger sections, using a 6mm (¼in) seam allowance. Then sew the sections together to complete the quilt top. Lightly press the seams to one side as you go, so that all the vertical and horizontal seams eventually lie in alternate directions.

## QUILTING

1 Smooth the backing, right side down, on a flat surface and centre the wadding on top. Centre the quilt top, right side up, on the wadding. Safety pin the three layers together in the usual way (see page 139).

2 Thread the sewing machine with either a contrasting or toning colour according to preference. Fit a darning foot, set the stitch length to zero and drop the feed dogs ready for free-motion quilting. Before you begin to stitch on the quilt, practise stitching around the leaf shapes on three layers of scrap fabric. Move the fabric under the needle as it stitches the thread to produce sketch-like lines around the shapes. Control the stitch length with the speed at which you move the fabric and aim for even stitches.

3 When you feel confident with the scrap fabrics, return to your quilt. Sew through the layers, loosely following the centre line and outline of each leaf shape to create a sketchy effect. You can sew from one leaf to the next and from one block to the next without stopping and starting, making a continuous line connecting all the leaves. The more you sew on the background fabric around a leaf, the more that leaf will puff up and stand out. Quilt as much or as little as you wish. The cut edges of the fabrics are left raw, to add to the textural qualities of the quilt.

4 Lightly press the quilt, using a pressing cloth to protect any delicate or glitzy fabrics. Check that the edges of the quilt top are straight and the corners are square. Trim the quilt top as necessary. Machine sew a line of stitches 6mm (¼in) in from the edges to give them added strength.

## FINISHING THE QUILT

Join the short ends of the binding strips to make one long strip to go right around the quilt. Attach the strip to make a double binding as described on pages 143–4. If you wish to display your quilt on a wall, attach a hanging sleeve following the instructions on page 145.

## QUILT CARE

If you display this quilt on a wall, it will not need washing. The occasional shake outside will be enough to keep the surface free from dust. If you have used many different kinds of fabric and would like to give the quilt a more thorough clean, then dry-cleaning is recommended.

## ADAPTING THIS DESIGN

■ Choose different colours to alter the whole tone of this quilt. For example, if the leaves are in soft greens against a background of pastel flower colours, you could create the look of a spring garden. Alternatively, leaves in vibrant reds and yellows on a background of dark fabrics would look very dramatic.

■ Try arranging the blocks in a different way. For example, you could have all the leaves lying in the same direction or piece the blocks to make a square, rather than a rectangle.

The ideas for this quilt seemed to emerge of their own free will while I was doodling. I love the simple shapes used by Matisse, so perhaps his influence started to take shape in these angels. I also wanted to use strong colours and these blues and purples make my angels very modern, while still exuding peace and harmony. It's amazing how the quilt took on a life of its own.

*Esther MacFarlane*

# Guardian angels

**SIZE**
**Finished quilt:** 92 x 112cm (36¼in x 44in)
**MATERIALS**
- 112cm-wide (44in-wide) cotton fabrics:
  - 1.25m (1¼yd) in navy (background)
  - 1.75m (2yd) in lavender (appliqué, backing and binding)
  - 30cm (12in) in purple (appliqué)
  - 50cm (20in) in royal blue (appliqué)
  - 20cm (8in) in electric blue (appliqué)
  - 50cm (20in) in pale olive (appliqué)
- 99 x 121cm (39 x 47in) lightweight needlepunched cotton wadding
- Sewing machine threads in black, lavender, purple, pale olive, royal and electric blue
- Basting thread in a contrasting colour

**Note:** use either metric or imperial measurements; they are not interchangeable

## CUTTING

- 1 rectangle, 94 x 116cm (37 x 46in), from the navy cotton (background).
- 1 rectangle, 99 x 121cm (39 x 48in), from the lavender cotton rectangle (backing).
- The remaining lavender cotton is for the binding, but do not cut this until after the quilt is otherwise complete.

## APPLIQUE

1 Smooth out the background fabric, right side up, on a flat surface. Measure and mark a 14cm (5½in) border in from each edge, using a quilter's pencil. Then divide this 66 x 88cm (26 x 35in) centre panel into four smaller panels, each measuring 33 x 44cm (13 x 17½in). Put this fabric to one side.

2 Using a pencil or fine permanent marker, trace the templates on pages 152–3 onto template plastic. Also transfer the instructions on each template. Carefully cut out the templates.

3 Referring to the quilt diagram on page 57, determine which appliqué shapes should be cut out from each colour of fabric. Smooth out the first fabric, right side down, on a flat surface and mark around the relevant template to make two shapes, leaving space for a 6mm (¼in) turning allowance. Then flip the template over and mark two more shapes in the same way, as mirror images. Mark out the other shapes on the relevant fabrics so that you have four from each template, two facing one way and two the other. Cut the shapes out, including the turning allowances.

4 Now lay the background fabric on a flat surface again. Referring to the quilt diagram, arrange the plastic templates in the top left-hand panel. Place the star slightly outside the lines of the rectangle, with the two smaller points facing inwards. Adjust the positions of the templates as necessary to find a balance. Mark around the templates with a quilter's pencil.

Quilter's tip *Specks of lint show up clearly on dark fabrics. Remove them by wrapping adhesive packing tape around your hand and rubbing it gently all over the fabric.*

5 Reposition the templates as mirror images in the top right-hand panel. Adjust them to align with the existing marked out design and then trace around them as before. Eventually you will need to mark out the final two panels as mirror images of the top two panels, but this can be done after the top two panels have been appliquéd to avoid the outlines rubbing off too soon.

6 Clip into the turning allowance around the curved edges and corners of the fabric shapes as necessary. Baste and then steam press the edges of the shapes under first if you wish or leave them to be needleturned later (see page 132).

7 Pin and baste each shape in the correct position on the background fabric. Using matching thread, slip stitch each shape to the background (see page 112) . Remove the basting threads. When all the shapes are applied to the two top panels, repeat the process on the two bottom panels.

8 Make sure any loose threads are fastened off and remove any lint. Remove any guidelines with a soft, damp cloth. Steam press the quilt top.

## QUILTING

1 Layer the backing, wadding and quilt top, and then safety pin them together in the usual way (see page 139). Thread the sewing machine with black thread on the top and lavender thread in the bobbin.

2 Following the guidance for curved line quilting given on page 136, quilt an outline close around each of the appliquéd shapes. Avoid starting and finishing with reverse stitches if this shows up too much on the background fabric. Instead, leave 10cm (4in) lengths of thread and fasten them off when the quilting for each panel is complete (see page 141). Then sew another line 6mm ($\frac{1}{4}$in) outside each of the first outlines.

3 Remove the quilt from the machine and lay it on a flat surface ready to mark the remaining quilting pattern with a quilter's pencil. Mark the next outline as a continuous line around all the appliquéd shapes, 1.2cm ($\frac{1}{2}$in) outside the existing quilting lines. Mark the next and the remaining lines 2.5cm (1in) outside each previous line, adjusting them so that they flow smoothly. Continue in this way until you have filled the background fabric, breaking the lines at the edges of the quilt as necessary.

4 Return the quilt to the sewing machine and quilt along each of the marked lines. Alternatively, use an adjustable quilting gauge so that you can sew the quilting without marking the lines first. Fasten off any loose threads and remove any guidelines as before.

## FINISHING THE QUILT

1 Check that the corners of the quilt are square and the edges are straight. Trim the quilt as necessary.

2 Take the measurements and cut enough strips of the lavender fabric to make a double binding, following the instructions on pages 143–4. Join the ends of the strips as necessary to make one long strip and then attach it to the quilt.

## QUILT CARE

If you make this quilt in cotton fabrics, it can be washed by hand in lukewarm water. Gently squeeze the excess water from the quilt and dry it flat, in the shade, outdoors. When the quilt is dry, tumble dry it on a cool cycle to fluff up the wadding.

## ADAPTING THIS DESIGN

■ Choose a different colour scheme for the fabrics. For example, you could combine bright colours to make a playmat for a baby.

■ Machine sew close satin stitch around the appliqué shapes, remembering to leave off the turning allowances.

■ Hand quilt the contour lines using thread in a colour that tones with both top and backing fabrics. For example, purple would work well with the colour scheme here.

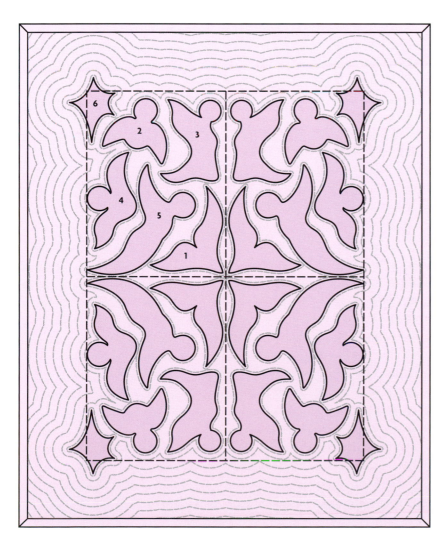

## KEY TO QUILT DIAGRAM

**1** and **6** = beige

**2** = electric blue

**3** = purple

**4** = lavender

**5** = royal blue

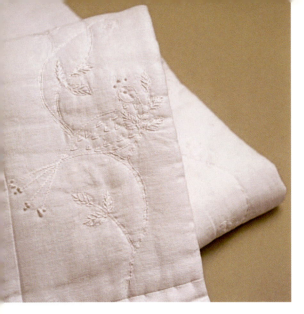

I love the idea of embroidery becoming a treasured heirloom and whitework still looks cool and elegant in stylish interiors today. The Swedish embroidery of the 1950s that inspired this quilt took a long time to stitch by hand, but here the sewing machine helps to speed up the work. The delicate design of exotic little birds among entwined branches makes a romantic quilt that would make a beautiful wedding present. *Karen Spurgin*

# White romance

**SIZE**
Finished quilt: 150 x 180cm (60 x 70in)
**MATERIALS**
■ 3.25m x 140cm-wide (3½yd x 54in-wide) linen in white
■ 3.7m x 112cm-wide (4¼yd x 44in-wide) cotton (backing)
■ 3.25m x 200cm (3½yd x 80in) lightweight polyester wadding
■ 6 skeins coton perlé No 5 in white
■ 2 balls coton perlé No 8 in white
■ Sewing machine thread in white
Note: use either metric or imperial measurements; they are not interchangeable

## CUTTING

■ Cut the linen into the following pieces, adding 6mm (¼in) seam allowances all round for each piece:
  ● 118 x 145cm (46 x 55in) for the main panel
  ● 2 side borders, each 17 x 145cm (7 x 55in)
  ● 1 top and 1 bottom border, each 17 x 118cm (7 x 46in)
  ● 4 corner posts, each 17 x 17cm (7 x 7in).
■ Cut 1 piece of wadding, 155 x 185cm (62 x 72in). Then cut the rest of the wadding into the same pieces as for the linen.
■ Cut the backing into 2 panels measuring 185cm (72in) long, but do not trim the width at this stage.

## TRANSFERRING THE DESIGN

1 There are two templates for this design, each one in two parts, on pages 150 and 151. Pieced together, the two parts for each template form one repeat. First piece together sheets of tracing paper or cut a length of greaseproof (waxed) paper just over half the length of the side borders. Trace the template for the side border at one end of the paper, matching up the overlapped sections as indicated and marking the repeat line. Then rotate the strip of paper by 180 degrees and trace the template again for the second repeat, matching it up to the first repeat. Draw around the design with permanent black marker to make sure you have a strong outline.

2 Now trace the template for the top and bottom borders onto one end of another strip of tracing or greaseproof (waxed) paper. This time, trace a reverse image of the template for the second repeat.

3 Fold each template in half both lengthways and widthways to find the centre lines. Do the same with each piece of linen for the borders and mark the centre lines a short distance from the edges with pins.

4 Lay the design pattern for the side border on a flat surface. Centre the linen for one of the side borders on top of the pattern. Place the linen wrong side up, because the design will be stitched from this side. Align the centre lines and pin the linen securely to the pattern. Working over a light box or other source of light and using a quilter's pencil or water-erasable marker, mark out the design on the linen fabric (see page 129).

5 Transfer the same pattern onto the linen for the other side border, but reversing the design from left to right. Transfer the second pattern onto the top border and then either flip it over or keep it the same way up for the bottom border, according to personal preference.

## STITCHING THE DESIGN

1 Prepare the coton perlé No 8 by winding it onto an empty cotton reel. Pop the reel onto the sewing machine and rewind the thread onto the machine bobbin in the usual way. Use sewing machine thread for the top thread and the ordinary presser foot. Set the machine to running stitch, with a stitch length of 2. Before you start on the quilt design, practise sewing a simple outline with these threads on a piece of scrap linen. Remember to sew with the wrong side of the fabric uppermost and to keep the fabric taut. Start sewing straightaway, rather than back-stitching, and fasten the threads off later. Check that the stitch tension is correct and that the coton perlé stitches make a clean line on the right side (underside) of the fabric.

2 Sew along all the outlines of the design. Complete each of the four borders in the same way. Pull any loose threads through to the wrong side and fasten them off. Lightly press the borders. Centre each border, right side up, over the top of the corresponding panel of wadding and baste the two layers together.

3 Complete the rest of the embroidery on the borders by hand with the coton perlé No 5, working through both the linen and the wadding. Stitch a French knot (see page 112), with two twists of thread around the needle, for each dot indicated on the eyes, crowns and tails of the birds. Use fly stitch (see page 112) for the feathers on the bird's bodies, as shown on the patterns. Embroider larger fly stitches to make the veins on the leaves and use running stitch (see page 110) to fill the stems.

4 Centre the main panel of linen over the corresponding piece of wadding and baste the two layers together. Using the coton perlé No 5, embroider clusters of one to four fly stitches about 10–15cm (4–6in) apart at random across the whole centre panel.

## PIECING AND LAYERING THE QUILT

1 Centre each square of linen for the corner posts, right sides up, on the corresponding square of wadding and baste them together well. With a 6mm (¼in) seam allowance, pin, baste and sew one corner post to each end of the top and bottom borders. Trim the wadding from the seams and, using a pressing cloth,

press the seams to one side. Sew the side borders to the centre panel in the same way. Finally sew the top and bottom borders and corner posts to the rest of the quilt top. Remove the basting stitches from the seams. Make sure that the corners of the quilt top are square and trim the edges as necessary.

2 Piece the two strips of backing, right sides together, with 6mm ($\frac{1}{4}$in) seams (see page 137). Press each seam to one side. Lay the backing, right side up, on a flat surface. Centre the quilt top, right side down, on the backing. Lay the remaining, large piece of wadding over the quilt top. Trim the three layers to the same size and pin and baste the edges together.

3 Using a walking foot and with the wadding on top, machine sew a 2.5cm (1in) seam around all four edges of the quilt, leaving a 50cm (20in) opening on the bottom edge. Trim the seam allowance and the excess fabric at the corners and remove all the basting stitches.

4 Turn the quilt right sides out, coaxing the corners out. Press the edges of the quilt. Pin, baste and slip stitch (see page 112) the opening together.

5 Baste the layers of the quilt together (see page 139). Quilt in the ditch (see page 136) along the seams on the quilt top. Fasten off any loose threads, remove the basting stitches and press the quilt.

## QUILT CARE

This quilt can be machine washed on a gentle cycle and dried outside on a windy day.

## ADAPTING THIS DESIGN

If you are going to make this quilt as a wedding present or want to add romance to your own bedroom, incorporate the relevant names or initials and wedding date into the design.

This whole cloth quilt is a glorious creation of colour and texture. The faux-felt surface is made by quilting down the luxurious fibres of wool, mohair and silk, and adding fascinating detail with other decorative yarns. This method makes it very easy to create a truly unique work of art. *Gillian Hand*

# Cocoon

## SIZE
**Finished quilt:** 102 x 115cm (40 x 45in)

## MATERIALS
- 1 x 1.5m (40 x 60in) cotton fabric (foundation)
- 1.1 x 1.6m (44 x 64in) water-soluble fabric
- 1 x 1.6m (40 x 64in) cotton fabric (backing and hanging sleeve)
- 1 x 1.5m (40 x 60in) low loft wadding of your choice
- 50cm (20in) cotton, silk or linen (binding)
- Fabric paints or dyes in assorted colours
- 500g (1lb) washable, unspun fibres of wool, mohair and silk in assorted shades
- Selection of different fancy yarns in assorted shades
- 2 x 500m (547yd) spools machine thread in contrasting or toning colours
- Basting thread in a contrasting colour

**Note:** use either metric or imperial measurements; they are not interchangeable

## PREPARING THE FOUNDATION

A cotton fabric has been recommended for the foundation, but any other fabric with a close weave such as linen or silk could also be used. First the foundation is dyed to add depth to the whole design and provide a complementary effect in case the background shows through the fibres and threads. To dye the fabric, either space dye it following the dye manufacturer's instructions or use the following method. Before you start on the whole quilt, read through all the instructions and make a small sample. This will give you the confidence to handle the larger piece.

1 Spread a sheet of plastic over a flat surface and lay the foundation fabric on top, right side up. Lightly spray the fabric with water so that the fabric paints will blend together and not leave harsh lines.

2 Begin to add colour to the foundation, applying two or three different shades of red paint in circular curves out from the centre. Fill in the spaces between the red and cover the rest of the foundation with paint in the full spectrum of colours, from yellows and oranges to greens, blues and purples. Use curving lines to reflect the red shapes and allow the colours to blend into each other.

3 When you have finished dyeing the fabric by either method, fix the colour according to the manufacturer's instructions and allow the fabric to dry thoroughly for at least 24 hours. Then press the foundation well.

## MAKING THE QUILT TOP

1 Lay the backing, right side down, onto a flat surface. Smooth it out and tape down the corners, midpoints and then the edges with masking tape to keep the fabric square and taut. Centre the wadding on top of the backing and smooth it out towards the edges. Centre the foundation fabric, right side up, on top of the wadding.

2 Working from the centre, begin to position the wool fibres on the foundation. Arrange them so that the colours complement the shades of dye on the fabric. Gradually cover most of the design, leaving some small areas where the foundation shows through. Gently tease out the fibres with your fingers to blend the colours together, creating a painterly effect.

3 When you have covered the design with the wool, add mohair and silk fibres in the remaining exposed areas until you have an even thickness over the whole design (although you could leave some areas of exposed foundation to be filled in at later stages if you wish). Tease the fibres out as before and mingle them with the wool. Stand back to look at the design and take the time to blend strands of varying thickness so that the colours gradually form a unified whole, rather than remaining within obvious boundaries.

4 When you are satisfied with the design so far, begin the next layering process. Select fancy yarns of varying thickness and texture, which complement the colours in the design. Arrange them randomly across the surface of the unspun fibres so that they are fairly evenly distributed and help to unify the whole composition. These yarns will add details of texture to the design, but don't add so many that the beauty of the unspun fibres is overwhelmed.

5 Centre a piece of water-soluble fabric over the whole design, so that it extends about 2.5cm (1in) beyond the edges. This will hold all the fibres and yarns in place while you are quilting. Using safety pins, pin all the layers together (see page 139), making sure that each pin goes all the way through to the backing. Place the pins 8–10cm (3–4in) apart.

## QUILTING

1 Decide whether to use threads in colours to match each area or to tone with the whole design. In Cocoon, matching thread was used and overlapped to blend the boundaries between different areas of colour.

2 Set the sewing machine up for free-motion quilting, with the stitch length at zero, attaching a darning foot and dropping the feed dogs. Begin to stitch a meandering pattern in the centre of the quilt, removing the safety pins as you secure the immediate area (for more detail on free-motion quilting, see page 116). The quilting can meander in any direction, crossing previous lines, but do take care not to make any tucks in the backing. Continue in the same way until you have securely quilted through all the layers with an even, but not very dense, distribution of stitches and removed all the safety pins. It is best to quilt over the whole quilt and then return to fill in areas in several stages because the water-soluble fabric is liable to disintegrate if stitches are packed too densely all at once.

3 Now return to the centre of the design and start to fill in areas with more quilting. Continue quilting out from the centre until the whole surface is fairly closely, but again not too densely, covered.

4 Stand back to look at the whole design and consider whether there are any areas that are not sufficiently secured to the foundation fabric or that need

to be filled with quilting. Return to these areas and continue quilting until you are satisfied with the design.

## FINISHING THE DESIGN

1 Trim away any excess areas of water-soluble fabric from around the edges. Place the whole quilt into a large sink or bath of cold water. Don't use hot water as all the fibres are liable to shrink at different rates and cause the whole quilt to pucker across the surface and buckle round the edges.

2 Leave the quilt in the water for approximately 30 seconds to allow the water to penetrate and the water-soluble fabric to dissolve. Rinse the quilt in fresh cold water several times until neither the water nor the textile feel sticky and there is no longer any foam in the water.

3 Squeeze the quilt with your hands to remove as much moisture as possible without wringing it. Give it a quick spin in a spin dryer if you have one. Lay the quilt on a large towel on a flat surface. Smooth out the surface and gently pull the edges into shape. Allow it to dry thoroughly and naturally.

4 Decide whether to iron the quilt or not. A light ironing will bring out the sheen of the silk fibres, smooth down the surface and flatten the quilt a little. If you want the textures to be more pronounced, do not iron the quilt.

## BINDING THE QUILT

1 Trim the edges of the quilt to straighten them and square up the corners. Measure along each edge to calculate the amount of binding needed. Don't worry if your quilt seems to have shrunk during the rinsing stage – this is intrinsic to the process and doesn't spoil the design.

2 Cut two 6cm (2½in) bindings the same length as the short sides. Cut the other two bindings the same length as the top and bottom edges, plus 6cm (2½in). Attach a 2.5cm (1in) square binding using the method on page 143.

3 If you wish to display your quilt on a wall, attach a hanging sleeve following the instructions on page 145.

## ADAPTING THIS DESIGN

Try limiting the colours you use to a palette that suits the decoration in the room where you want to display the quilt.

## QUILT CARE

Lightly brush the surface of this wall hanging to remove dust. Dry clean or gently hand wash it in warm water if necessary.

This quilt celebrates the creativity of the Ndebele women in the region north of Pretoria, in what was once the southern Transvaal. They continue a long tradition of painting the walls of their homesteads and love using dark toning colours, with black and a touch of white. Symmetrical geometric shapes inspired by familiar household items, such as razor blades, are very popular. The women also make dazzling beadwork, so black beads seemed the perfect embellishment for the design. *Terry Pryke*

# Spirit of Ndebele

## SIZE
**Finished quilt: 91 x 123cm (36 x 50in)**
## MATERIALS
■ 112cm-wide (44in-wide) cotton fabrics:
  • 1.4m (1½yd) in terracotta (background)
  • 50cm (20in) in mottled brown
  • 30cm (12in) in grape
  • 20cm (8in) in cream
  • 2.8m (3yd) in black (backing and binding)
  • 50 x 50cm (20 x 20in) in smoke, beige, coffee and terracotta
■ Scrap fabrics in tan, purple and blue
■ 2m x 100cm-wide (2¼yd x 40in-wide) lightweight iron-on interfacing
■ 105 x 140cm (42 x 55in) needlepunched cotton wadding
■ 15m x 15mm-wide (16½yd x ⅝in-wide) satin ribbon in black
■ 1.5m x 10mm-wide (1⅔yd x ⅜in-wide) satin ribbon in black
■ Sewing machine threads to match the fabrics
■ Small packet of black beads
■ Sewing thread in black
■ Basting thread in contrasting colours
**Note:** use either metric or imperial measurements; they are not terchangeable

## PREPARING THE FABRICS

1 Fold the terracotta background in half lengthways and lightly press the fold. Repeat the process widthways to find the centre of the fabric and its edges, to help you to position the appliqué shapes later.

2 Tape together pieces of card or paper to make one 90 x 130cm (36 x 52in) sheet for the pattern. Using the grid method on page 128, enlarge the design outline on page 148 onto the prepared sheet so that the outline measures 81 x 120cm (32 x 48in). Transfer all the labels on the diagram on page 75 to your pattern.

3 Lay the pattern out on a flat surface. Place the interfacing, adhesive side down, on top of the pattern and secure the two together. Holding the interfacing so that it does not shift and using a fine permanent marker, trace around each shape on the pattern to make a separate template for each one. Label each shape on the non-adhesive side of the interfacing. Cut out all the shapes.

4 Referring to the quilt diagram on page 69, determine which shapes should be cut from each of the fabrics. Put your iron on a cool setting, with no steam. Working with matching appliqué fabrics and interfacing shapes, smooth the fabric, right side up, on the ironing board and place the interfacing shapes, adhesive side down, on top, leaving enough space for a 6mm (¼in) turning allowance around each shape. Place a sheet of paper over the interfacing and very lightly iron to fix the interfacing to the right side of the fabric (you will need to remove the interfacing later). Use the same method to lightly bond the interfacing shapes to all the relevant fabrics (you could replace the interfacing with freezer paper if you prefer). Cut all the shapes, adding the turning allowance to each one. Clipping into the allowance as necessary, press the turnings under on each of the shapes.

5 If you wish, trace the pattern for the centre panel onto the right side of the terracotta background fabric using a quilter's pencil (see page 129). Alternatively, keep the pattern to use as a guide for positioning the appliqué.

## APPLIQUE

1 Pin and then baste the turning allowance under around shape X. Carefully remove the interfacing. Centre shape A on top of shape X. Pin, baste and slip stitch (see page 112) it in place. Remove the basting stitches you no longer need. Turn the background X over to the wrong side and carefully remove the excess cream fabric inside the outline of shape A, leaving a 6mm ($\frac{1}{4}$in) allowance (see page 132). Draw a line with a chalk powder wheel or quilter's pencil 1cm ($\frac{3}{8}$in) inside the outline of shape A.

2 Using a beading needle, secure a length of black thread and bring it up to the right side of the fabric. Pick up one bead and slip it along the thread to lie on the surface of the fabric on the drawn outline. Take the needle down through the fabric close to the other side of the bead and then anchor the bead with another stitch through it. Bring the needle back up one stitch-length away, following the outline. Pick up another bead and anchor it by making a back stitch knot (see the illustration opposite and page 110). Continue attaching the beads with back stitch to make a continuous row. Fasten off securely when you reach the beginning again. Attach a second row of beads in the ditch between shapes A and X.

3 Pin and then baste the turning allowance under around shape C. Carefully remove the interfacing. Position shapes B1 and B2 on shape C. Pin, baste and slip stitch them in place. Then pin and baste shape X in position. Remove the basting stitches you no longer need. Carefully remove the interfacing and then the excess fabric from the reverse side, as before.

4 Pin and baste the 15mm ($\frac{5}{8}$in) ribbon around shapes B1 and B2, mitring it at the corners and tucking the ends under shape X. (The method for mitring a double binding on pages 143–4 can be adapted for mitring the ribbon.) Slip stitch the ribbon in position. Then slip stitch shape X in position and remove the basting stitches. Appliqué the 15mm ($\frac{5}{8}$in) ribbon around shape X in the same way.

5 Follow the same methods to appliqué shape C to D and then to the terracotta background, and the pairs of corner triangles together. Slip stitch the 15mm ($\frac{5}{8}$in) ribbon around the edges of the inner corner triangles. Then appliqué the corner triangles to the background and stitch 15mm ($\frac{5}{8}$in) across the long edges of the outer triangles. Finally, apply the 15mm ($\frac{5}{8}$in) ribbon around the outer edges of shapes C and D.

6 Appliqué together the shapes for the long edges of the design. Attach a single row of black beads in the ditch between the semicircular and half-cross shapes. Slip stitch the 10mm ($\frac{3}{8}$in) ribbon around the outer edges of shapes H and Q. Finally, appliqué these edge shapes in position on the background and apply the 15mm ($\frac{5}{8}$in) ribbon around the outer edges of shapes J and P. Remove any remaining basting stitches and gently steam press the back of the quilt top.

## QUILTING

1 Trim the quilt top to measure 91 x 130cm (36 x 52in). Cut a 140cm (56in) length of the black fabric for the backing. Layer the backing, wadding and quilt top

together using safety pins (see page 139). Trim the backing and wadding to leave an extra allowance of 5cm (2in) all round the quilt top.

2 Starting in the centre of the quilt and using a matching colour of thread, machine quilt in the ditch (see page 136) on both sides of the ribbon around shape A.

3 Smooth out the quilt, right side up, on a flat surface ready to mark out the rest of the quilting patterns. Using a chalk powder wheel or quilter's pencil, mark out a 2.5cm (1in) crosshatch pattern on shape C. Quilt this pattern in matching thread. Referring to the quilt diagram, mark out and quilt first the geometric patterns in shape D and then the outline quilting on the background.

## FINISHING THE QUILT

1 Fasten off any loose threads. Checking that the corners are square and the sides straight, trim the quilt to make a rectangle aligning the outer edges of the appliquéd triangles, including an extra seam allowance of 6mm ($\frac{1}{4}$in) all round.

2 Take the measurements and cut four 15cm (6in) strips of the black fabric to make a double binding, following the instructions on pages 143–4.

## QUILT CARE

If you make this quilt in cotton fabrics, it can be washed by hand in lukewarm water. Gently squeeze the excess water from the quilt and dry it flat, in the shade outdoors.

## ADAPTING THIS DESIGN

■ Try adding more beading, in black or other complementary colours.

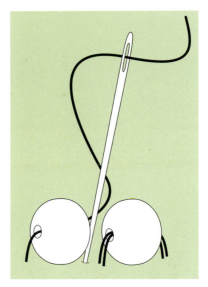
*Sewing the beads on with back stitch*

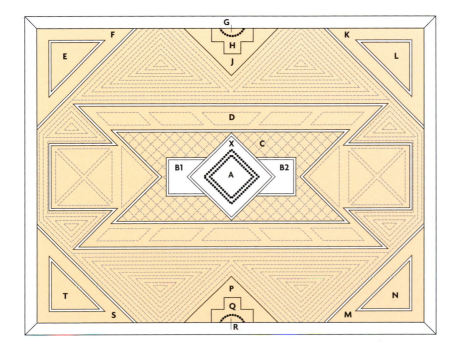

## KEY TO QUILT DIAGRAM

**A**, **B1** and **B2** = terracotta

**C** = grape

**D** = mottled brown

**E**, **G**, **L**, **N**, **R** and **T** = tan, purple and/blue according to preference

**F**, **K**, **M** and **S** = smoke

**H**, **Q** and **X** = cream

**J** = beige

**P** = coffee

I think that quilts provide a focus for reflection and relaxation to feed our souls, rather than just warm our bodies. So I like making wall hangings that are theatrical, opulent or even rather dreamy. Using mother-of-pearl buttons from my vintage collection has made me feel particularly attached to this quilt. The buttons, and the block-printed patterns, certainly enhance the strong graphic look of the black and cream linen. *Diane Groenewegen*

# Forms of attachment

## SIZE

**Finished quilt:** 92 x 128cm (36 x 50in)

**Finished block (12):** 19 x 19cm (7½ x 7½in)

## MATERIALS

- 112cm-wide (44in-wide) fabrics:
  - 5m (5½yd) medium-weight black linen (blocks and binding)
  - 1.5m (1⅔yd ) medium-weight cream linen (sashes)
  - 1.5m (1⅔yd) open weave cotton (backing)
- 1m (1yd) interfacing
- 1m (1yd) paper-backed fusible web
- 1.5m x 112cm (1⅔yd x 44in) wool wadding
- Fabric printing paste or acrylic paint (with textile medium) in bright white
- Foil in silver
- Cotton sewing machine thread in black, cream, white and two greys
- Cotton crocheting thread in red or black
- 150 mother-of-pearl buttons in various sizes
- Coton perlé No 5 in black
- Coton perlé No 8 in red
- Basting thread in a contrasting colour
- 15m x 12mm-wide (16½yd x ½in-wide) black bias binding

**Note:** use either metric or imperial measurements; they are not interchangeable

## CUTTING

- 12 squares, each 20 x 20cm (8 x 8in), from the black linen (blocks).
- 2 strips, each 10 x 132cm (4 x 52in), from the black linen (side bindings),
- 2 strips, each 10 x 97cm (4 x 38in), from the black linen (top and bottom bindings).
- 12 squares, each 19 x 19cm (7½ x 7½in), from both the interfacing and the fusible web (block foundations).
- Cut the cream linen, wadding and cotton backing to 92 x 128cm (35 x 50in) each, for the three main layers of the quilt.

## PRINTING THE BLOCKS

The blocks must be printed and then the foil applied before the machine stitching is started. Refer to the diagram on page 72 to help you if you wish to copy the exact design of Forms of Attachment. Alternatively, you could use these ideas to create your own patterns.

1 Lay one square of black linen, right side down, on the ironing board. Following the manufacturer's instructions, centre the fusible web on the linen and bond it in place. Then bond a square of interfacing to the back of the fusible web. This will leave a 5mm (¼in) allowance round the edge of the linen. Repeat this process on the rest of the squares to give a firm basis for the printing and machine embroidery.

2 If you are going to make printing blocks, keep the patterns relatively simple. On Forms of Attachment, home-made blocks of fine corrugated cardboard stuck onto polystyrene created simple parallel lines in 4cm (1½in) squares, 4 x 10cm (1½ x 4in) rectangles and diamonds to contrast with the freer forms made by two sizes of hair scrunchy. A little bit of luck was added with a number 3 on a bought rubber stamp!

3 Protect your work surface with a sheet of plastic and then put an old blanket or towel on top. Use the fabric printing paste or mix the acrylic paint with

## KEY TO QUILT DIAGRAM

**1** A grid of 9 corrugated squares, with 12 silver foil squares used as diamond blocks in between; small buttons attached with black thread on each foil square.

**2** Curving lines of machine stitch in white and two shades of grey; tiny buttons radiate from one large button, all attached with red thread.

**3** A big diagonal cross of large scrunchy circles with diagonal lines of white machine stitch in between; small buttons stitched with black thread in the centres of the circles.

**4** A grid of curving machine-stitched lines in white; medium buttons in alternate void areass, attached with red thread.

**5** Diagonal lines of corrugated rectangles, with 3s and silver foil on top; embellished with a few tiny buttons sewn on with black thread.

**6** Diagonal lines of corrugated diamonds with lines of white machine stitches in between; tiny buttons attached with red thread, which is knotted, with the ends left long.

**7** An upright cross of small scrunchy circles, with a machine-stitched grid in white; small buttons stitched in the centre of each circle with black thread.

**8** Five horizontal lines of machine stitch in white; a diamond of 21 large buttons attached with red thread.

**9** Two sets of four lines form a diagonal cross of machine stitch in white and two shades of grey; small buttons are attached with black thread.

*(Key continues on page 73.)*

textile medium so that it will adhere to the linen and spread some on a sponge in a shallow tray. When you load the printing block or scrunchy with paint, dab the excess off on some spare paper or fabric until there is just enough paint to make an impression. Print each block of black linen according to the key or your own choice. Then leave them on a flat surface to allow the paint to dry thoroughly. Using a pressing cloth, press the blocks with a hot iron to fix the printing.

4 Now apply the silver foil to some of the blocks. On Forms of Attachment, 2.5cm (1in) squares of foil were used. First cut the fusible web into squares and bond this to the blocks where you want the foil to appear. Then, using a pressing cloth, bond the foil to each of the fusible web squares.

## STITCHING THE BLOCKS

Machine stitch across the blocks with automatic stitches after they have been printed and the foil has been applied. Then stitch on the buttons.

1 Draw any guidelines and stitching lines that you need with a quilter's pencil. Try out the automatic stitches on your machine on a scrap piece of linen. Choose about six to use on the blocks. Use white and the two shades of grey machine thread. Stitch steadily to ensure that you make good straight or smooth curving lines.

2 Embellish the blocks with pearl buttons in a variety of sizes. Stitch them on with either the black machine thread or the red crocheting thread. Some can be stitched on in the conventional way, but add interesting detail to others by stitching over the buttons to make straight lines and crosses.

## PIECING THE QUILT

1 Fold the cream linen down the centre, matching the two long sides, and finger press the fold. Open the fabric out and lay it, right side up, on a flat surface with one of the short sides at the top.

2 Using a pastel quilter's pencil, mark a line down the pressed central line from the top and bottom edges. Then mark a horizontal guideline 13cm (5in) down from the top edge and another the same distance up from the bottom edge.

3 Pick up block 2 and find the midpoints along the top and bottom edges. Aligning the midpoints on the block with the central line on the cream linen, butt the top edge of the block up to the top guideline. The block should be right side up. Pin and baste the block in position.

4 Mark another guideline across the cream linen along the edge of the block, making sure that it is parallel with the top guideline. Then mark another parallel line 8cm (3¼in) below that. Position block 5 to butt up to the last guideline in the same way as before. Pin and baste it in place. Repeat the process to position blocks 8 and 11, leaving the 8cm (3¼in) strips of cream linen in between.

5 Now mark guidelines for an 8cm (3¼in) strip of cream linen on each side of the central row of blocks. Position the remaining blocks, butting them up to the guidelines, and pin and baste them in place.

## QUILTING

1 Trim the quilt top to give an 8cm (3¼in) border of cream linen round the edges, with a further seam allowance of 6mm (¼in). Cut the backing and wadding to the same size. Layer the quilt and baste it for hand quilting (see pages 138–9).

2 Place the bias binding along all the edges of the cream strips. Pin, baste and stitch them in position. Embellish the intersection of each grid line with a large cross stitch (see page 112) in red crocheting thread. Finally, hand quilt along the strong directional lines in the patterns on the blocks, using the black coton perlé.

## FINISHING THE QUILT

1 Remove all the basting stitches and press the quilt top, using a pressing cloth to avoid damaging the buttons and foil. Trim the backing and wadding to the same size as the quilt top.

2 Trim the two side binding strips so that they are the same length as the quilt sides. Attach the side bindings (see square binding on page 143). Trim the top and bottom strips to length, including the side bindings and a seam allowance. Attach these strips to complete the binding.

3 If you wish to display your quilt on a wall, attach a hanging sleeve following the instructions on page 145.

## QUILT CARE

This is a heavy quilt and is not suitable for washing. Take it to a reputable dry-cleaner.

## KEY TO QUILT DIAGRAM
*(Continued)*

**10** A diagonal grid of lines in alternating red and white machine stitches; small buttons are sewn on the intersections with red thread.

**11** A grid of 16 small corrugated squares, alternating vertical and horizontal lines, with the four central and the four corner squares overprinted with square diamonds; large buttons are attached to the four central shapes with black thread.

**12** A grid of nine large scrunchy swirls, with another grid of red machine stitch in between; small buttons are sewn to the inner end of each swirl with red thread.

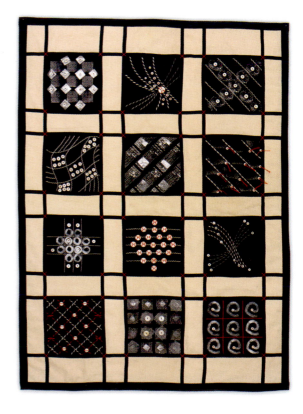

Woollen cloth has a very natural beauty, whether it is dyed in subtle earthy shades or strong bright colours. You can see the texture of each individual thread, so it is hardly surprising that they produce a very tactile fabric. The main tweed fabric in this quilt inspired the choice of colours for the other blocks and the tassels, to make the perfect throw for a picnic or a wrap to snuggle into on a boat. *Hikaru Noguchi*

# Tasselbrick

**SIZE**

**Size**
Finished quilt: 200 x 200cm (79 x 79in)

**MATERIALS**
■ 140cm-wide (54in-wide) woollen fabrics:
 • 75cm (29½in) flannel in red
 • 75cm (29½in) flannel in green
 • 75cm (29½in) flannel in beige
 • 2.1m (2½yd) tweed in mixed colours
■ 4.1m x 150cm-wide (4 ½yd x 60in-wide) cotton print (backing)
■ 4.1m x 150cm (4 ½yd x 60in) wadding
■ Basting thread in a contrasting colour
■ Sewing machine thread in a complementary colour
■ Knitting wool in complementary colours (tassels)

Note: use either metric or imperial measurements; they are not interchangeable

## CUTTING

Follow the shape sizes given in the key on page 77.

■ 4 of shape F; 8 of shapes A and C; 12 of shape D; and 16 of shape E in the red flannel.
■ 4 of shapes D and E; 8 of shapes B, C and F; and 12 of shape A in the green flannel.
■ 4 of shape D; 8 of shapes A, E and F; and 12 of shape B in the beige flannel.
■ 4 of shape A; 8 of shape E; and 12 of shapes B, C and F from the mixed tweed.
■ 4 strips, each 22 x 205cm (8¾ x 81in), of the mixed tweed (borders).
■ Cut the backing fabric in half widthways, but do not trim the width of the backing or the wadding at this stage.

## PIECING THE QUILT TOP

1 Start by piecing together the top row of shapes for the centre panel, following the quilt diagram on page 77. Pin, baste and machine sew the shapes, wrong sides together, using a 1cm (⅜in) seam allowance. Piece together each of the other rows in the same way. Remove the basting threads and press all the seams open. Then join the rows together in the same way, following the diagram.

2 Smooth the centre panel, right side up, on a flat surface. The right side displays all the seam allowances, which are a feature of this design. Check that the edges are straight and the corners are square, and trim the panel as necessary. Put a pin at the midpoint along each edge and measure across the middle of the quilt from pin to opposite pin to give you the basic lengths of the side, top and bottom borders. Add seam allowances of 1cm (⅜in) all round to these measurements.

3 Mark the midpoint along one long edge of each border. Place one of the side borders along one long side of the centre panel and pin the midpoints, right sides together. Pin the ends of the border in place and then, aligning the

edges, pin the rest of the seam. Baste the seam, easing the edges to fit. Sew the border in place with a 1cm (³⁄₈in) seam, starting and stopping exactly 1cm (³⁄₈in) away from the adjacent edge. Attach the other three borders in the same way. Then remove the basting stitches and press the seam allowances towards the borders.

4 Mitre the corners of the borders, working on the wrong side (see pages 126–7). Machine sew the mitred seams together. Trim the seam allowances. Remove any remaining basting stitches and press the seams open.

## LAYERING THE QUILT

1 Again, make sure that the edges of the quilt top are straight and the corners are square. Trim the quilt top as necessary. Piece the two strips of backing, right sides together, with 1cm (³⁄₈in) seams (see page 137). Press each seam to one side.

2 Lay the backing, right side up, on a flat surface. Centre the quilt top, right side down, on the backing. Centre the wadding over the quilt top. Pin and baste all three layers together. Then trim the backing and wadding to the same size as the quilt top.

3 Using a walking foot and with the wadding on top, machine sew a 1cm (³⁄₈in) seam around all four edges of the quilt, leaving a 50cm (20in) opening on the bottom edge. Trim the seam allowance and the excess fabric at the corners. Remove all the basting stitches. Turn the quilt right sides out, coaxing the corners out fully.

4 Press the open edges of the quilt. Pin, baste and slip stitch (see page 112) the opening together. Remove the basting stitches.

## FINISHING THE QUILT

1 Safety pin the layers of the quilt together in the usual way for machine quilting (see page 139). Machine sew a running stitch 1cm (³⁄₈in) in from all the edges. Quilt in the ditch (see page 136) along the border seams.

2 Make as many tassels as you wish to add to the quilt top, randomly choosing the colours of yarn to match or contrast with the fabrics. Cut a rectangular piece of card with the long sides the same measurement as the length of the finished tassel, plus an extra 1.5cm (⅝in). Cut a tying thread about 20cm (8in) long and lay this along the top of the card. Wrap your chosen yarns around the card and the tying thread until the tassel has the appropriate bulk (see the illustration, left). Tie the ends of the tying thread tight around the wrapped threads with a double knot. Without cutting the thread or yarn, slide the wrapped yarn off the card. Wrap another length of yarn tightly around the tassel a short distance from the top and knot it. Then, cut through the wrapped loops at the opposite end to the tying thread. Thread the ends of the binding yarn into a needle with a large eye and take them into the centre of the tassel. Trim the ends of the tassel so that they are the same length.

3 Use the tying threads to attach the tassels to the quilt, sewing them through all the layers and fastening them off on the backing side.

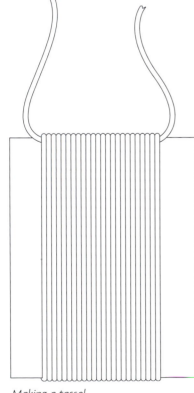

*Making a tassel*

## QUILT CARE

If you make this quilt in woollen cloth, it is not recommended for washing. Instead, take it to a reputable dry-cleaner.

## ADAPTING THIS DESIGN

■ Try using a thicker wadding and hand tie the layers of the quilt together.

■ You could use other fabrics, such as cotton corduroy, for a similarly rustic feel, although it might be better to keep the seam allowances on the wrong side as they will fray more easily than wool.

## KEY TO QUILT DIAGRAM

**Shape A** = 6 x 10cm (2³⁄₈ x 4in)

**Shape B** = 10 x 10cm (4 x 4in)

**Shape C** = 10 x 14cm (4 x 5¹⁄₂in)

**Shape D** = 10 x 18cm (4 x 7¹⁄₈in)

**Shape E** = 10 x 26cm (4 x 10¹⁄₄in)

**Shape F** = 10 x 42cm (4 x 16¹⁄₂in)

**R** = red

**G** = green

**B** = beige

**T** = tweed

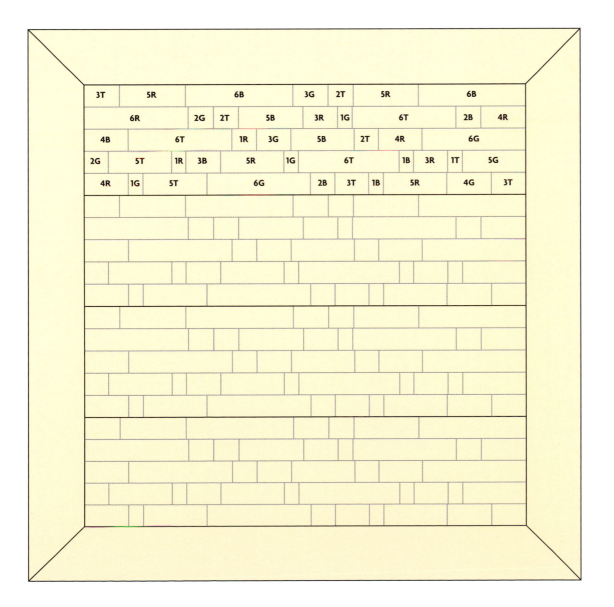

This contemporary scrap quilt features the warm, earthy-coloured batiks that I had in my stash of fabrics. I needed only to add a plain background in the warm putty colour found in many of the prints to create a subtle and stylish effect. The modern cut-and-sew technique produces repeat blocks that look very effective en masse. *Alison Schwabe*

# Earthspring

**SIZE**
**Finished quilt:** 120 x 150cm (48 x 60in)
**Finished block (80):** 15 x 15cm (6 x 6in)
**MATERIALS**
■ 18 x 23cm (7 x 9in) x 40 printed cotton fabrics
■ 4.5m x 112cm-wide (5yd x 44in-wide) cotton fabric (background, binding and backing)
■ 130 x 160cm (52 x 64in) low to medium loft wadding of your choice
■ Sewing machine and hand quilting threads in toning colours
■ Gütermann Skala in grey or clear nylon monofilament
**Note:** use either metric or imperial measurements; they are not interchangeable

**Quilter's tip** *You could cut six rectangles of fabric for this quilt from one fat quarter or three rectangles from a fat eighth.*

## CUTTING

■ For the background, cut 7 strips, each 23cm (9in) wide. Then cut each strip into 6 rectangles, 18cm (7in) long. This gives you 42 rectangles, enough fabric for 84 blocks – you will hardly notice piecing 4 extra ones and they'll give you a degree of choice when you put all the blocks together.

■ Cut the cotton prints into 42 rectangles, each 18 x 23cm (7 x 9in), for the contrasting parts of the blocks.

■ 5 strips, each 5cm (2in) wide, across the width of the binding fabric.

■ Do not cut the backing or wadding until the quilt top has been finished.

## PIECING THE BLOCKS

All the blocks are cut freehand with a rotary cutter and then pieced together by alternating plain and printed fabrics. This produces a number of 'vertical' seams which, when sewn together, reduce the width of each block. The blocks are then are trimmed into squares. If this is the first time that you have tried cutting freehand with a rotary cutter, it is a good idea to practise the technique on some spare fabric until you feel confident.

1 Place one rectangle of plain fabric on the cutting mat and put a rectangle of printed fabric directly on top, both right sides up. Don't worry if they are not exactly the same size, but do make sure that one short and one long edge align perfectly with each other.

2 With the rotary cutter and starting at about 7.5cm (3in) from one short edge, cut a gently curving line through both layers of fabric from one long edge to the other. Cut two to four more lines in the same way. Separate the fabrics and alternate the plain, then the printed pieces like two jigsaw puzzles, ready to reconstruct as two separate blocks. Eventually, one set will look like a negative image of the other.

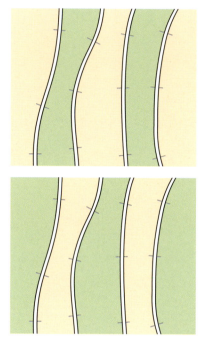

*Matching the two sets of fabrics to make two blocks*

3 With a pencil, tailor's chalk or fine water-erasable marker, mark a few registration marks along the curved edges on neighbouring pieces of fabric. The more curved the line, the more marks you will need to help you match the seams.

4 Pick up two neighbouring pieces of fabric for one block. (Leave the others safely to one side so that the order is not disturbed.) Place the two pieces right sides together and pin them through the registration marks. Pin the rest of the seam together. Sew a 6mm (¼in) seam, removing the pins as you go. Sew the rest of the pieces together to complete the first block.

5 Press the seams towards the darker fabric. Check that you are happy with the block. You might wish to add another piece to divide a wide area of one fabric, although do consider whether there is the space to do this before cutting the fabric.

6 When you are satisfied, place the block on the cutting mat and trim it to a 16.2cm (6½in) square, which includes further seam allowances. Repeat the same process to complete 84 blocks.

7 Lay all the blocks out on a flat surface, organised in ten rows of eight blocks. Swap any of the blocks around, including the four spare ones, until you are satisfied with the composition.

8 Sew the blocks together to make up the rows. Press the seams towards the darker fabrics. Then sew the rows together to complete the quilt top. Press these seams as before and then gently press the right side of the quilt top.

### QUILTING

1 Cut two 82 x 130cm (33 x 52in) strips of the backing fabric. Piece the backing together following the instructions on page 137 and using 6mm (¼ in) seam allowances. Press the seam to one side.

2 Trim the edges of the quilt top and make sure that they are square. Layer the quilt and safety pin the layers together in the usual way for machine quilting (see page 139).

3 Machine quilt in the ditch (see page 136) between each block using Gütermann Skala, which does not catch the light and becomes practically invisible, or the clear nylon monofilament.

4 Hand quilt curving contours across each block. The contours could follow the shapes of the pieced fabrics and also weave across the wider areas of plain fabric. You can use long and short stitches on a purely decorative quilt, but if it is going to be used on a bed, keep the stitches short so that they do not get caught by fingernails or jewellery.

### FINISHING THE QUILT

1 Trim the backing and wadding to the same size as the quilt top. Join the short ends of the binding strips as necessary to make one long strip to go right around the quilt. Attach the strip to the quilt and make a double binding, in this case will be 1cm (³⁄₈in) wide, following the instructions on pages 143–4.

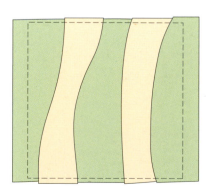

*Trimming a pieced block to the correct size*

$2$ If you wish to display your quilt on a wall, attach a hanging sleeve following the instructions on page 145.

## ADAPTING THIS DESIGN

■ For the background fabric, try using a traditional cream calico or another plain fabric in a colour that appears in at least several of your prints.

■ The number of blocks in this design can easily be adapted to make a smaller or larger quilt.

■ Experiment with a smaller size of finished block. This could offer interesting possibilities for using small pieces of fabric called charm squares – so often collected, but not as often used.

Traditional embroidery has inspired me since my grandmother left her treasured pieces to me. When I started to look around in antique markets, car boot sales and charity shops, I found beautifully worked tray cloths, pillowslips and table mats. Often the fabric was stained and worn, but the stitching was exquisite and unharmed. Piecing them together in this quilt has made it possible to preserve these embroidered flowers. *Karen Spurgin*

# Oxfam flowers

## SIZE

**Finished quilt:** 155 x 190cm (62 x 75in)

## MATERIALS

■ Pre-washed embroidery pieces (to make 4 strips of 6.2 x 195cm (2½ x 77in)

■ 112cm (44in) wide fabrics:
- 2m (2¼ yd) linen in cream
- 50cm (20in) raw silk in green
- 40cm (16in) duchess satin in pink
- 30cm (12in) silk chiffon floral print
- 3.9m (4⅓ yd) cotton in blue and white stripes (backing)

■ 160 x 195cm (64 x 77in) lightweight polyester wadding

■ Sewing machine thread in toning colours

■ Basting thread in a contrasting colour

**Note:** use either metric or imperial measurements; they are not interchangeable

## CUTTING

■ Begin by cutting up the pieces of embroidery. Cut each piece individually, to give a finished width of 5cm, plus two 6mm (¼in) seam allowances. The length of each piece must also include the seam allowances, but will vary depending on the particular embroidery design. However, it may not be possible to cut out a whole motif or centre it on the piece of fabric – cutting through a motif adds to the charm of this quilt of recycled fabrics and wastes less of the precious embroidery. Cut enough pieces to make 4 strips, each 195cm (77in) long.

■ 1 piece, 36.2 x 195cm (14½ x 77in), from the cream linen (centre panel).

■ 2 strips, each 31.2 x 195cm (12½ x 77in), from the cream linen (side panels).

■ You need to cut enough of the pink satin, green silk and floral print to make 4 strips of each, 195cm (77in) long. Cut 4.2cm (1¾in) strips of the pink satin, 6.2cm (2½in) strips of the green silk and 3.2cm (1¼in) strips of the floral print across the width of each fabric.

■ 2 pieces, each 195cm (77in), from the striped cotton (backing). Do not trim the width of the backing at this stage.

## PIECING THE STRIPS

1 First piece together the four strips of embroidery patches. Pick out the pieces of embroidery at random. Pin, baste and then machine sew each one to the next with a 6mm (¼in) seam to make the first strip. Remove the basting stitches and press all the seams to one side.

2 Make the second strip in the same way, but press the seams in the opposite direction. Machine sew these two strips together along the length. Remove the basting stitches and press the seam allowance to one side. Make the other pair of strips in the same way.

Piece together the strips of pink satin, green silk and floral print to make four 195cm (77in) long strips of each one. Join these narrow strips of fabric to each strip of embroidery with 6mm ($\frac{1}{4}$in) seams. First machine sew a strip of pink duchess satin along both long edges of each embroidery strip. Then attach a strip of the floral print on each side of the two panels, followed by the green silk.

Using 6mm ($\frac{1}{4}$in) seams, machine sew a pieced strip to each long edge of the centre panel of cream linen. Finally, attach the other two panels of cream linen to the outer edges to finish the quilt top. Remove all the basting stitches and press all the seams to one side.

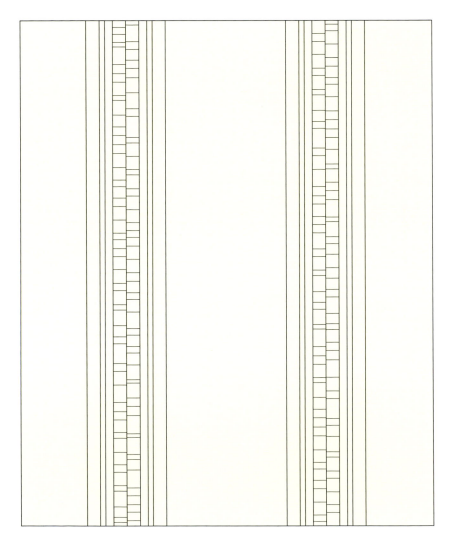

## LAYERING THE QUILT

1 Check that the edges of the quilt top are straight and the corners are square. Trim the quilt top as necessary.

2 Piece the backing together, with 6mm (¼in) seams, following the instructions on page 137. Press each seam to one side. Lay the backing, right side up, on a flat surface. Centre the quilt top, right side down, on the backing. Pin and baste them together. Then trim the backing to the same size as the quilt top. Lay the wadding over the quilt top. Pin and baste the three layers together and trim the wadding to the same size.

3 Using a walking foot and with the wadding on top, machine sew a 2.5cm (1in) seam around all four edges of the quilt, leaving a 50cm (20in) opening on the bottom edge. Trim the seam allowances and the excess fabric at the corners and remove all the basting stitches.

4 Turn the quilt right sides out, coaxing the corners out fully. Press the edges of the quilt. Pin, baste and slip stitch (see page 112) the opening together. Remove the basting stitches and press the quilt.

## QUILT CARE

Because this quilt combines very different fabrics, it is not suitable for washing. Instead, take it to a reputable dry-cleaner.

## ADAPTING THIS DESIGN

If you have enough pieces of embroidery, make cushions to match your quilt.

Travelling in the desert of western Australia, I fell in love with its amazing landscape. The panels of this quilt, with their rich shades of silk, were inspired by the exquisite effects of the light at dawn, noon and dusk. The softly-fringed edges suggest the shimmering heat and add movement, which draws the eye to the stitched detail, reminiscent of the insects, birds and seeds that survive in this burning landscape. *Diane Groenewegen*

# Desert dreaming

**SIZE**
Finished quilt: 83 x 120cm (33 x 48in)

**MATERIALS**
- 30–50cm (12–20in) lengths of silk dupion fabric in 21 different shades
- 130cm-wide (52in-wide) fabrics:
  - 90cm (37in) fine cotton voile (foundation fabric)
  - 90cm (37in) silk dupion (backing)
- 90 x 130cm (37 x 52in) wool wadding
- Coton perlé in colours to complement the fabrics
- Silk embroidery floss in deep red
- Basting thread in a contrasting colour
- Transparent machine thread

**Note:** use either metric or imperial measurements; they are not interchangeable

## SELECTING THE FABRICS

It is not important, and probably not possible, to reproduce the exact shades of silk used in Desert Dreaming. Instead, collect together fabric for three colour schemes that suggest the mood of the panels. The shades in the left panel range from cream to beige and include pale gold and apricot; those in the centre focus on rich gold and burnt orange, with gold and lime for an exotic touch; the final panel is a collection of rich brown and bronze, with a little peach and copper.

Although each panel has a particular colour scheme, be prepared to use some of the shades from each panel on the others. This links the panels together and adds extra life to each one.

## CUTTING

- Cut all the silk fabrics for the quilt top into 30cm-wide (12in-wide) strips. Do not cut the strips up until later when you decide on the depth of each band of fabric.
- Cut both the cotton voile and the wadding into 3 strips, 30cm (12in) long.

## PIECING THE QUILT

1 Lay the strips of voile side by side on a flat surface. Lay strips of wadding on top and baste this foundation for each panel together. It helps to work on all the panels at the same time to ensure that they complement each other well.

2 Decide on the first silk fabric to go across the bottom of one of the panels. Lay it in place on the panel and decide how deep it should be. Remove it from the panel and, using dressmaker's shears or a rotary cutter, cut it on a straight horizontal line. Reposition it on the panel.

3 Now choose the second fabric, which will lie on top of the first. Fray the bottom edge of the fabric by gently pulling the horizontal threads away until

*The finished decorative cross stitch*

you have a significant fringe. With a small comb, gently tease the fringe out. Then spray it with starch and comb it out again while it is still damp. Using the setting for silk, iron the fringe immediately. Pin the fabric in position on the panel.

On Desert Dreaming, some of the fringes stayed straight, but others relaxed to give some interesting variations. Both are reminiscent of the desert grasses, some of which stand tall while others get blown by the breeze.

4 Continue to compile the fabrics for each panel, varying the depth, fringing the bottom edge and placing each new fabric on top of the previous one. Remember to use a few fabrics from the other two colour schemes in each panel. Pin each fabric in place on the panel as you go.

5 In some places, you may decide to use a wide strip of fabric and have one or two others with frayed top and bottom edges laid on top of it. In others, you may wish to use a strip with the edges turned under. Press a 6mm (¼in) turning to the wrong side of the fabric on the top and bottom edges of these strips before pinning them in place on the panel.

6 When you are satisfied with the composition of each panel, baste the fabrics in place on each foundation.

## QUILTING

1 A quilting hoop is not recommended for this quilt because of the risks of damaging the frayed edges and tearing the wadding. It is quite easy to keep the narrow panels taut with your hands as you work. Quilt through the layers of silk, voile and wadding using your collection of coton perlé threads. The choice of which colour and stitch to use can be completely personal, but first complete the basic quilting to make sure that all the loose edges of fabric are stitched down. In Desert Dreaming, the colours were chosen to match the tone of the fabric or relate to a neighbouring strip.

2 Slip stitch the edges that are turned under in place (see page 112). Attach frayed edges with one or two rows of running stitch (see pages 110–11). Work rows of parallel running stitch in horizontal or diagonal directions, or in gently curving contours, on some of the deeper strips of fabric. Leave other deeper strips without stitching until the panels are pieced together so that the stitch lines can be worked across all three panels to help unite them visually.

3 Add to the detail by embroidering herringbone stitch (see page 113) and a decorative cross stitch on a few of the strips. To stitch the cross stitch (see the illustration above), (a) make a large basic cross stitch (see page 112); (b) make two long stitches on each side of the first stitch; (c) make two long stitches on each side of the second stitch; (d) make a vertical stitch to tie down the previous stitches from the top to the bottom intersection; (e) make a short horizontal stitch to tie down the vertical stitch and the first basic cross stitch.

4 To complete the stitching, cut some small squares of silk fabric and fray all four edges of each one. Attach these squares with one cross stitch each in random drifts across the panels.

5 Carefully remove all the basting threads. Gently press the right side of the fabric using a pressing cloth. Complete the other two panels in the same way, making sure that they all complement each other.

## ASSEMBLING THE QUILT

1 Pin and baste the three panels together along the long edges with a 12mm (½in) seam, through all three layers. Check that none of the frayed edges are trapped in the seams and tease the fringe out if this is the case. Machine stitch the panels together and press the seams open. Then use a pressing cloth to press the right side of the quilt top.

2 Examine the stitch detail on the quilt and decide where to add quilting lines to link one panel to the next. In Desert Dreaming, gently curving lines were stitched across some of the deeper strips in colours that enhanced the relationship between the panels and suggested the contours of landscape.

3 Lay the backing on a flat surface and centre the quilt top on top of it, right sides together. Trim the edges so that they are straight and the corners are square. Then pin and baste the layers together.

4 Machine stitch a 12mm (½in) seam around the edges, leaving a 50cm (20in) opening on the bottom edge. Remove the basting stitches and trim the excess fabric and wadding on each corner. Turn the quilt right sides out, carefully coaxing the corners out fully. Pin, baste and slip stitch the open edges together. Remove the basting stitches and, using a pressing cloth, press the edges.

5 Safety pin the layers of the quilt together (see page 139) and machine sew down each vertical seam with transparent thread, removing the pins as you go.

6 This quilt is not really recommended for use on a bed as the stitches and frayed edges might easily get caught by fingernails or jewellery. If you wish to display your quilt on a wall, attach a hanging sleeve following the instructions on page 145.

## QUILT CARE

This silk quilt with its frayed edge detail is quite delicate, so washing by hand is not recommended. Instead, take the quilt to a reputable dry-cleaner.

## ADAPTING THIS DESIGN

Use shades of silk and thread to reflect your feelings about a landscape in your own environment at different times of the day.

I designed this quilt to make a very graphic statement on a sofa or armchair, like a piece of modern art. Dramatic pleats are sewn down to create a series of waves that flow across the quilt to create textural impact, while the suedette adds a soft, comfortable feel that is perfect to snuggle up to. Just like a cup of good coffee – a very satisfying quilt! *Angelina Pieroni*

# Cappuccino waves

**SIZE**

Finished quilt: 120 x 120cm (47 x 47in)

**MATERIALS**

■ 5.5m x 154cm-wide (6yd x 60in-wide) suedette in beige

■ 1.5m x 154cm-wide (1²⁄₃yd x 60in-wide) suedette in brown (backing and binding)

■ 130 x 130cm (51 x 51in) cotton wadding

■ Sewing machine thread in two toning colours

■ Basting thread in a contrasting colour

**Note:** use either metric or imperial measurements; they are not interchangeable

## CUTTING

■ 1 piece, 130cm (51in) square, from the brown suedette (backing).

■ 4 strips, 5cm (2in) wide, from across the width of the brown suedette (binding).

■ 42 strips, each each 5 x 130cm (2 x 51in), from the beige suedette (quilt top). You may find it easier to use a rotary cutter than scissors for this.

■ 36 bias strips, each 7 x 130cm (3 x 51in), from the beige suedette (quilt top). Lay the fabric on a flat surface. Align the straight cut edge across the width with the adjacent long edge and press the resulting diagonal fold so that you can use it as a guide for cutting the bias strips.

## PIECING THE QUILT TOP

This quilt is made in six horizontal panels. Each panel is made up of seven straight and six bias strips of the beige suedette.

1 Taking care that the fabric does not twist, fold each of the bias strips in half lengthways, wrong sides together. Press the folds in place. Pin and then baste the two long raw edges together. Using a walking foot and toning thread, machine sew a 6mm (¼in) seam along each strip to hold the edges together. Remove the basting stitches.

2 To start the first panel, take one straight and one folded bias strip. Align the long raw edges of the bias strip with one long raw edge of the straight strip, right sides together. Pin, baste and then machine sew them together with a 1cm (½in) seam. Place another straight strip on top of the bias strip, right sides together. Pin and baste all three strips together, so that the bias strip is trapped between the two straight strips. Machine sew them together along exactly the same seam line as before. Remove all the basting threads. Open the fabric out, so that the bias strip lies flat on top of one of the straight strips and press the seam allowances under the other straight strip.

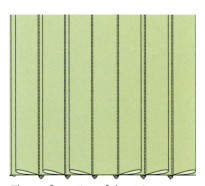

*The configuration of the strips on one of the panels*

3 Pin, baste and sew another bias strip to the second straight strip, right sides together. Repeat the previous process to trap the second bias strip with another straight strip. In this way, join together a total of six pairs of straight and bias strips, with one additional straight strip at the end. Remove all the basting stitches.

4 Press the seam allowances in towards the straight centre band, so that the pleats fan out from the middle in two sets of three. Using a toning colour,

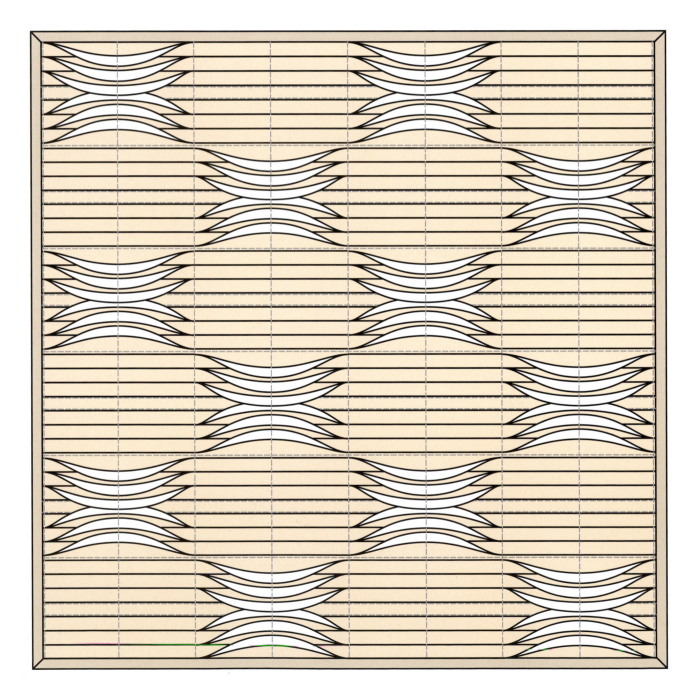

machine sew close to each seam to keep the allowances in place. Using a pressing cloth, steam press the panel.

5 Make the other five panels in the same way. Square up and trim each panel. Then join the panels together along the long edges, with a 1cm (½in) seam. Press these new seams to one side.

## QUILTING

1 Layer and pin the backing fabric, wadding and quilt top in the usual way for machine quilting (see page 139). Use plenty of safety pins to secure the layers together because the suedette does tend to migrate easily. Make sure that all the pleats lie in the correct directions.

2 Thread the machine with two colours, the one in the needle to tone with the quilt top and the other on the bobbin to tone with the backing. Quilt in the ditch (see page 136) along both edges of each centre band and then along each seam joining the panels together.

3 Fold the quilt in half at right angles to the previous quilting lines. Mark the midpoints on the edges with pins and then mark a straight line across the fabric to join the midpoints. Machine quilt along this line. Mark out four more lines, two at 30cm (12in) intervals on each side of the first line. Quilt along these lines too.

4 Now pin the pleats into the wave pattern. Starting with the top left block, fold the bottom three pleats upwards and pin them in place. Then pin the top three pleats downwards, so that the bottom one overlaps the top pleat of the other set. Do the same on the next two alternate blocks. Mark a straight line, centred between the quilting lines on each side. Machine quilt along the line, removing the safety pins just before you reach them.

5 Repeat this process so that the next set of waves start on the second block down from the top edge. Alternate this pattern until you complete the waves and create a chequerboard effect.

## FINISHING THE QUILT

Make sure that the corners of the quilt are square and the edges straight. Trim the backing and wadding to the same size as the quilt top. Join the short ends of the binding strips as necessary to make a strip to go right around the quilt. Follow the instructions on pages 143–4 to make a double binding. Using a damp cotton pressing cloth, lightly steam press the quilt.

## QUILT CARE

Sponge any small stains with dry-cleaning fluid, but take the quilt to a reputable dry-cleaner if necessary.

## ADAPTING THIS DESIGN

After you have sewn the pleats flat, choose which sections to fold down to make the waves and create your own different design.

My mother, Machiko, has been collecting kimono fabrics for a number of years. Because she has treasured them for so long, I wanted to make a very special quilt. Most of the fabrics I chose have rich, vibrant colours, which I find very seductive and uplifting. I added tiny tassels and embroidered flowers on the plain colours to give a feel of sheer luxury to this quilt. *Hiroko Aono-Billson*

# Machiko's gift

## SIZE

Finished quilt: 240 x 250cm (95 x 99in)

## MATERIALS

- Selection of plain and patterned fabrics (quilt top)
- 8.2m x 112cm-wide (9yd x 44in-wide) plain fabric (backing)
- 240 x 250cm (95 x 99in) wadding
- Silk sewing machine thread in a selection of colours to complement the fabrics
- Polyester thread in red
- Basting thread in a contrasting colour
- Stranded embroidery threads in two colours to complement the fabrics

**Note:** use either metric or imperial measurements; they are not interchangeable

*Quilter's tip Plan and draw your design to scale on graph paper so that you can cut the fabrics to size, adding a seam allowance all round, without the need for templates.*

## DESIGNING THE QUILT

1 Tape sheets of paper together to make one 240 x 250cm (95 x 99in) piece. Lay the sheet out on a flat surface. Mark a 10cm (4in) border around each outer edge. Then divide the central area into four horizontal strips. They do not need to be of equal depth.

2 Start to draw out your design for the patchwork in the central area, copying the diagram on page 97 if you wish. Alternatively, you could make up your own similar design, in which case you might like to sketch it out on graph paper first. Leave the bottom strip as one plain area. On Machiko's Gift, this bottom strip is bright red, which gives visual weight to the design.

3 Divide the top three strips into smaller panels. The size and shape of these panels is a matter of preference. However, make sure that groups of panels make up larger blocks of different shapes and sizes. This will make them easier to piece together and the resulting continuous seams will help the shapes flow into each other.

4 Decide where the fabrics you want to use should go on the design. Plan the different fabrics, especially the plain colours, evenly across the design to give it balance. Colour the design or label each shape to indicate the different fabrics.

5 When you are satisfied with the balance of the design, clearly number each pattern piece. Make a tracing of each patchwork shape on the design. Label each template with its number and your choice of fabric.

## CUTTING

- Cut out all the pieces for the quilt top, using the templates and adding a 6mm (¼in) seam allowance all round.
- Cut 3 strips from the backing fabric, each 274cm (109in) long. Do not trim the widths at this stage.

## PIECING THE QUILT

1 Sew the patchwork pieces together, making sure that you stitch accurately along the seam lines. Start by joining pieces that will make up into blocks, so that you can go on to sew the blocks together into larger units with the minimum number of seams. Press all the seams towards the darker fabrics as you go, using an appropriate heat setting. When you have finished piecing all the strips, sew them together with a 6mm ($\frac{1}{4}$in) seam. Press the quilt top.

2 Mark the embroidery design outlines on the right side of the plain panels on the quilt top ready to embroider them later (see page 129). Enlarge the templates on pages 152–5. You will need to piece the smaller ones together in two halves if you do not have access to an A3 copier and the larger template on pages 152 and 153 will need piecing together on a number of sheets. Draw around the main lines on the templates with a permanent black marker to make them stand out clearly. Lay the quilt over a light source and using a quilter's pencil, mark the design outlines in position.

## QUILTING

1 Prepare the backing by joining the three lengths with 6mm ($\frac{1}{4}$in) seams down the long edges. Press the seams to one side. Trim the backing so that it measures 264 x 274cm (105 x 109in). Pin a 2cm (1in) turning to the wrong side along all the edges of the backing. Baste the turning in place.

2 Smooth the backing out, right side down, on a flat surface. Centre the wadding on top of the backing so that there is a 10cm (4in) border of fabric all round. Position the quilt top, right side up, on top of the wadding to give a 10cm (4in) border all round. Baste the layers together in the usual way (see pages 138–9).

3 In keeping with Japanese traditions for making futons, and using the embroidery thread, hand tie the layers of the quilt together at the corners of each patchwork piece (see page 141). Also tie across the bottom strip, avoiding the areas to be embroidered later. Use 10cm (4in) lengths of embroidery thread in a colour to match the border. Make the tying stitches between 0.5 and 1cm ($\frac{1}{4}$–$\frac{1}{2}$in) long and trim the ends of the ties to a consistent length.

## FINISHING THE QUILT

1 Fold the backing to the front of the quilt along the side edges of the wadding. Pin and baste the edges in place. Then repeat the process on the top and bottom edges. Slip stitch the edges of the corners in place to keep them neat (see page 112) . Use an automatic machine stitch to sew along the inside edges of the broad border. Remove all the basting stitches, except those in the plain bottom strip of fabric.

2 Thread your machine with silk thread in a colour to complement the fabric. Fit a darning foot if necessary and lower the dog feeds ready to start free-motion embroidery. Stretch one of the areas for embroidery in a hoop or keep the fabric taut with your hands as your work. Embroider around the outlines of the

design, stitching smoothly and taking care not to catch the quilting ties. Then fill in the spaces with a few more free-flowing lines. Complete the other embroidery designs in the same way. When you have embroidered the bottom strip, remove any remaining basting stitches.

3 To finish the embroidery, make several French knots in the centre of each of the flowers (see page 112). Wind the thread around the needle about 12 times for each knot.

4 Finally, make a series of plaited tassels. Cut strips of different fabrics, about 1.5–2 cm (½–¾in) wide. Leaving the edges raw, choose three strips and knot them together at one end. Plait the strips to the desired length and then cut them, leaving a fringe. Make a knot in the fringed end. Then repeat the process with the same strips or a different combination to make more tassels. Carefully stitch the tassels to the quilt, taking care not to stitch through to the backing. On Machiko's Gift, thirteen tassels were used.

## QUILT CARE

This quilt is not suitable for washing. Instead, take it to a reputable dry-cleaner.

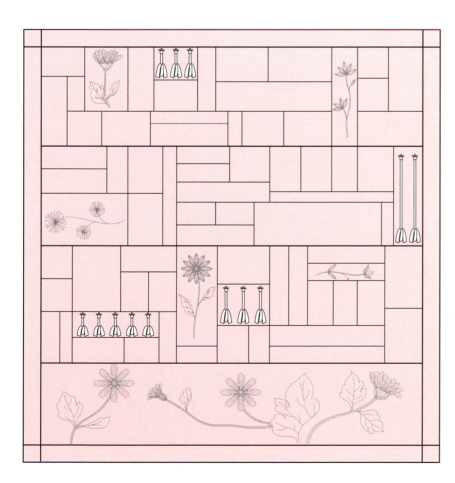

My love of flowers and bright colours seems to burst into life on this quilt. The rather retro look is my interpretation of the flower power era of the 1960s and was inspired by the fields of poppies that blanket the hills of Tuscany in springtime. I hope you enjoy the spirit of joy in this design. *Terry Pryke*

# Poppy fields

## SIZE

Finished quilt: 154 x 188cm (60 x 74in)

## MATERIALS

- 112cm-wide (44in-wide) cotton fabrics:
  - 7.5m (8¼yd) in white (centre panel, outer borders and backing)
  - 50cm (20in) in black (appliqué)
  - 50cm (20in) in red (appliqué)
  - 50cm (20in) in orange (appliqué)
  - 50cm (20in) in crimson (appliqué)
  - 50cm (20in) in pink/orange (appliqué)
  - 50cm (20in) in shocking pink (appliqué)
  - 2m (2¼yd) in dark green (inner borders and binding)
  - 0.25m (10in) in bright green print (appliqué)
  - 0.6m (24in) in lime green solid (appliqué and leaf frame)
- 165 x 200cm (65 x 78in) wadding
- 3m x 100cm-wide (3¼yd x 40in-wide) lightweight iron-on interfacing
- Basting thread in contrasting colours
- Sewing machine thread in colours to match the appliqué fabrics
- Quilting thread in white and red
- Stranded cotton embroidery thread in colours to match the flowers and leaves

**Note:** use either metric or imperial measurements; they are not interchangeable

## CUTTING

- 1 piece, 82.2 x 117.2cm (32⅜ x 46⅛in), from the white cotton (centre panel).
- 2 strips, each 31.2 x 121.2cm (12¼ x 47¾in), from the white cotton (outer side borders).
- 2 strips, each 31.2 x 146.2 cm (12¼ x 57½in), from the white cotton (outer top and bottom borders).
- 2 strips cut across the width of the fabric, 175cm (69in) long, from the white cotton (backing).
- 2 strips, each 3.2 x 121.2cm (1¼ x 47¾in), from the dark green cotton (inner side borders).
- 2 strips, each 3.2 x 86.2cm (1¼ x 34in), from the dark green cotton (inner top and bottom borders). Leave the rest of the dark green cotton for the binding.
- 2 bias strips, each 141.2 x 2cm (55⅝ x ¾in), from the lime green cotton (leaf frame).
- 2 bias strips, each 106.2 x 2cm (41⅞ x ¾in), from the lime green cotton (leaf frame).
- enough 3.5cm-wide (1½in-wide) bias strips of lime green cotton to make 4m (4⅓yd) for the flower stems.

## PREPARING THE FABRICS

1 Tape together pieces of card or paper to make one 170 x 200cm (67 x 78in) sheet for the pattern. Using the grid method on page 128, enlarge the design outline on page 147 onto the prepared sheet so that the outline measures 150 x 185cm (59 x 72¾in). Transfer all the labels on the design outline to your pattern.

2 Lay the pattern out on a flat surface. Place the interfacing, adhesive side down, on top of one of the flowers. Holding the interfacing so that it does not shift and using a fine permanent marker, trace around the outline of the flower petals. Label the shape on the non-adhesive side of the interfacing. Then trace around the outline of the flower centre to make a separate shape and label that too. Trace and label all the flowers and centres in the same way. Cut out all the shapes.

3 Referring to the quilt diagram on page 102, determine which shapes should be cut from each of the fabrics. Put your iron on a cool setting, with no steam. Working with matching appliqué fabrics and interfacing shapes, smooth the fabric, right side up, on the ironing board and place the interfacing shapes, adhesive side down, on top, leaving enough space for a 6mm (¼in) turning allowance around each shape. Place a sheet of paper over the interfacing and very lightly iron to fix the interfacing to the right side of the fabric (you will need to remove the interfacing later). Use the same method to lightly bond the interfacing shapes to all the relevant fabrics (you could replace the interfacing with freezer paper if you prefer).

4 Cut out all the shapes, adding a turning allowance of 6mm (¼in) to each one. Clipping into the allowance as necessary, press the turnings under on each of the shapes.

5 If you wish, trace the pattern for the centre panel onto the right side of the corresponding panel of white fabric, using a pastel quilter's pencil (see page 129). Alternatively, keep the pattern to use as a guide for positioning the appliqué shapes by eye.

## PIECING THE CENTRE PANEL

1 Carefully remove the interfacing from the front of the inner centres and the black centres of the flowers. Then pin and baste each of the inner centres to the corresponding black centre, both right sides up. Using thread in matching colours, slip stitch each pair of shapes together (see page 112). Remove the basting stitches. Turn the shapes over to the wrong side and remove the excess of black fabric inside the outlines of the inner centres, leaving a 6mm (¼in) allowance, so that they will puff up on the finished quilt (see page 132).

2 Remove the interfacing from each of the main poppy shapes. Pin and baste each flower centre onto the corresponding flower shape, both right sides up. Slip stitch each pair of shapes together and then remove the basting stitches. Remove the excess flower fabric from inside the outlines of the black centres in the same way as before.

3 Press a 6mm (¼in) turning under along both long edges of the lime green bias strips for the flower stems. Cut the bias strips to give the correct length for each stem on the pattern, adding a 6mm (¼in) allowance at each end.

4 Smooth out the white centre panel, right side up, on a flat surface. Pin and baste the appliqué shapes in position. Using thread in matching colours, slip stitch first the stems and then the flowers in place. On flower 1, stitch the petals to within 1.2 cm (½in) of the panel seam allowance, so that you can finish stitching them in place over the inner border later. Remove the basting stitches.

## PIECING THE BORDERS

1 Mark the midpoint of each side of the centre panel and also the midpoint of each of the dark green strips for the inner borders. Pin and then baste each border to the centre panel, right sides together, matching the midpoint markings.

Using matching thread, machine sew the borders in place, following the instructions for mitring the corners on pages 126–7. Remove the basting stitches and then press the seam allowances towards the green fabric.

2 Again, mark the midpoints on both the green borders and the white outer borders. Matching the midpoints, pin and baste the two side outer borders in place. Then machine sew them together. Attach the top and bottom borders across the edges of the centre panel and the side borders in the same way. Remove the basting stitches and press the seam allowance towards the green fabric.

3 Pin, baste and slip stitch the loose petals of flower 1 in place across the inner and outer borders. Then prepare the border flowers and their centres ready for appliqué as you did with those for the centre panel.

## PIECING THE LEAF FRAME

1 Using a fine permanent marker, trace the leaf template on page 146 onto template plastic. Then cut the shape out. Place the template right side down on the wrong side of the bright green fabric and using a pencil, mark out 65 leaves, allowing a 6mm (¼in) turning allowance all round each shape.

2 Smooth out the lime green fabric on a flat surface and place the marked bright green fabric on top, right sides together. Pin the two fabrics together through the centre of each leaf shape. Cut out the shapes, including the turning allowance and leaving the pins in place.

3 Using matching green thread, machine sew all round the outline on each leaf shape. Trim the turning allowances to 3mm (⅛in). Very carefully make a 1cm (⅜in) slit down the centre of the lime green side of each leaf. Gently turn each leaf right sides out through this slit. Use a needle to help you make the points sharp. Finger press the seams so that the leaves lie flat.

4 Smooth out the quilt top on a flat surface. Measure out and mark the leaf frame with a sharp pencil, 10cm (4in) outside the inner dark green border. Fold the strips of lime green fabric for the leaf frame in half lengthways and press them lightly. Mark the midpoints on each strip and each side of the leaf frame.

5 Line up the cut edge of one of the longer strips along the pencil line for one of the sides of the frame, matching the midpoints right sides together. Pin and baste the strip in position. Using a running stitch and a 3mm (⅛in) seam allowance, sew along the strip up to 6mm (¼in) from each end. Remove the basting stitches. Lightly press the strip back over to cover the seam and pin it in place. Then slip stitch along the folded edge. Repeat the same process on the opposite side, and then along the top and bottom edges of the frame, trimming back the seam allowances at the ends and neatly tucking in the corners so that they are square.

6 Referring to the quilt diagram, place the leaves approximately 7cm (2¾in) apart around the frame, including one at each corner to cover the joins. Pin and then baste along the centre line of each leaf, leaving the sides free to create a three-dimensional effect.

7 Using two strands of the green embroidery thread, work whipped back stitch (see page 113) along the centre line of each leaf to create a vein. Start the back stitch at the base of the leaf and finish 6mm (¼in) from the tip. Remove the basting stitches. With the same colour, whip over the back stitches, taking care not to stitch into the fabric.

## FINISHING THE OUTER BORDER

1 Using two strands of red and one strand of red/orange cotton embroidery thread, work five or seven whipped spider's webs (see page 113) of different sizes in the centre of each of the flowers for the outer border.

2 Referring to the quilt diagram, pin and then baste the flowers around the border. Using matching thread, slip stitch the flowers in place. Then remove the basting stitches to complete the quilt top.

## QUILTING

1 Gently steam press the back of the quilt top, taking care that the appliquéd leaves do not get bent out of shape. Piece the fabric for the backing together in the usual way (see page 137). Layer and safety pin the quilt together (see page 139).

2 Starting in the centre of the quilt and using matching colours of thread, quilt in the ditch (see page 136) around each of the appliquéd shapes in the centre panel, including the stems and both centres of each flower. Continue the lines around the petals into the centre of each flower.

3 Using white thread, outline quilt around the stems at 2cm (3/4in) intervals. Where the lines around one stem start to meet those around an adjacent stem, sew the ends of one set of lines up to the outer line of the neighbouring set.

4 Working outwards and using white thread, quilt in the ditch on both sides of the inner dark green border. Using matching threads, quilt in the ditch around the flower centres and petals. Finally, quilt a cross-hatched grid at 3.5cm (1 3/8in) intervals across the outer border.

## FINISHING THE QUILT

Fasten off any loose threads. Check that the corners of the quilt are square and the sides straight. Trim the quilt as necessary. Take measurements for the binding across the midpoints of the quilt. Cut four 9cm-wide (3 1/2in-wide) strips of the dark green fabric to make a square binding, following the instructions on page 143.

## QUILT CARE

If you make this quilt in cotton fabrics, it can be washed by hand in lukewarm water. Gently squeeze out the excess water and dry the quilt flat, in the shade, outdoors.

## ADAPTING THIS DESIGN

■ Try other colours of fabric to make different flowers or keep the red and green poppies but put them on a dark background.

■ Machine appliqué the shapes using close satin stitch, remembering to leave off the turning allowance.

# Techniques and templates

# Estimating yardage

The amounts of fabric you need for each of the quilts in this book are given in the panel at the beginning of the project. However, if you want to adapt one of them or design your own, you will have to estimate how much fabric you need. Many quilters can't resist buying gorgeous fabric as and when they see it, building up quite a stash that they can pick and choose from rather like using an artist's palette. That's tempting, but can be quite expensive. So for your first quilt, it's reassuring to calculate what you need and know that you won't run out of fabric to finish your masterpiece.

## QUILT DESIGNS

Traditional quilts are made of three layers. The quilt top can be put together in a great variety of ways involving

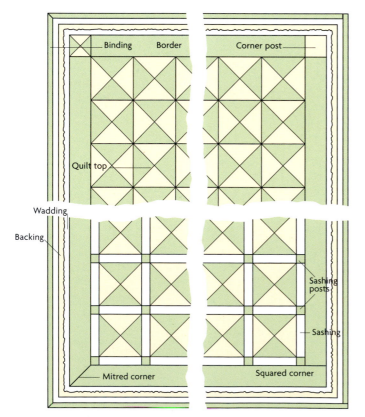

*The different parts of a typical quilt*

patchwork, appliqué or a quilted design on its own. Patchwork blocks are often interspersed with strips of fabric called sashes and many quilt tops have wide borders around the central design. Lines of quilting stitches trap a layer of wadding between the quilt top and a fabric backing, and the raw edges are finished with a binding.

## QUILT SIZES

The approximate finished size of each quilt in this book is given at the beginning of the project. However, many of the quilts, especially those based on repeated blocks, can be made in different sizes to suit your own requirements. If you are making a quilt for a particular bed, consider whether you wish to have a small decorative coverlet or a full size bedspread, including whether you want it to draw up over the pillows and hang to the floor all round the bed. Measure up the dimensions with the bed fully made and the pillows in position.

*Quilter's tip If you find it hard to visualize the size of quilt that will look best, spread a sheet over the bed and pin it up until you have found the perfect size.*

## PATCHWORK QUILT TOP

If your quilt top is basically one piece of fabric (a whole-cloth quilt), perhaps with an appliquéd design, calculate the amount of fabric you need in the same way as for the backing (see page 107).

Calculations for a patchwork quilt top need a pencil and paper – and a little more patience. For all your calculations, work with a shorter fabric width than the width of new fabric, to allow for any shrinkage and for removing the selvedges. For example, for 112cm (44in) fabric, work with a width of 100cm (40in).

1 Draw your patchwork design to scale on graph paper, including the sashing and borders. Colour the design in, using a different colour to represent each different fabric. Count up the number of different shapes in each colour.

As a simple example, you might have eight triangles in two different types of fabric in each of 20 blocks. Therefore your sketch will make an invaluable reference for you to use while you are making the quilt and, with the calculations you have made, will also provide a guide to yardage for future quilts.

2 Starting with one shape, work out how many will fit across the width of the fabric. Remember to add enough to allow for the seams of 6mm/¼in all round each of the shapes. Next divide the total number of that shape by the number that fit across the width. For example, if you want a total of 160 triangles and 12 fit across the width, you will need 14 times the depth of one triangle, plus allowances. To make it easier you could try doing this exercise on paper or alternatively you could work with templates on a piece of fabric – whichever you find easiest. Do the same for the other shapes in the same fabric and add the yardages together. Then proceed with the shapes for the other fabrics.

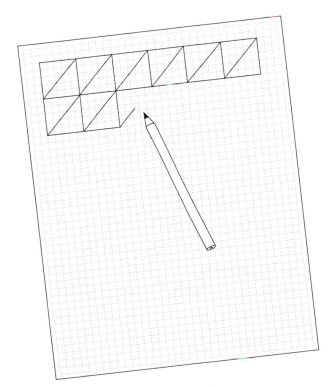

*Working out how many of the same shape will fit across the width of the fabric*

## SASHES AND BORDERS

1 The amount of fabric you need for these straight shapes on the quilt top is easy to calculate. Measure the finished length and width of each piece. For each piece, add seam allowances all round, plus an extra 5cm (2in) on the length.

2 Sketch a cutting plan on graph paper, so that the shapes can be cut out along the straight grain. Although some short sashes may fit across the width of the fabric, most will only fit along the length of the fabric, so it is best to plan them all out this way. Start by placing the longest lengths. Working down in size, place the other shapes. The total yardage is then easy to calculate. Use any excess fabric for some of the patchwork or appliqué pieces.

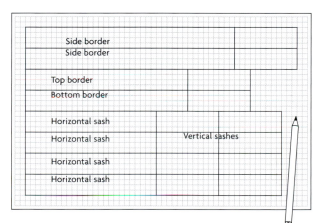

*Planning the yardage for sashes and borders*

3 In some circumstances you may wish to cut some of the shorter sashes and the top and bottom borders across the width of the fabric, for example when you want to take a nap into consideration or keep a pattern running in the same direction down the quilt. However, never cut sashes or borders on the bias.

## BACKING

Add 10cm (4in) to the length and width of the finished quilt. If the quilt is wider than the fabric, calculate how many widths of fabric you will need so that the seams can be placed symmetrically. A large quilt may need two or three widths. Multiply the length of the quilt, plus the allowance, by the number of widths needed to give the total amount of fabric required.

## BINDING

1 Add together the length and width of the finished quilt and then double that figure to give the total perimeter measurement. Then add 50cm (20in) to allow for finishing the ends and mitring the corners.

2 Binding strips are often 6.5cm (2½in) wide and can be cut on the straight or cross grain or on the bias. One square metre (yard) of 112cm (44in) wide fabric gives about 12m (13yd) of bias or 14m (15yd) of straight binding.

## APPLIQUE

Sort the appliqué pieces into groups of shapes that need to be cut from different fabrics. Plan them out on paper or on a piece of fabric, using their widest measurements and adding 6mm (¼in) turning allowance. Estimate the total yardage in a similar way to patchwork. Small appliqué shapes can also often be cut from scraps of fabric left from other projects.

## WADDING

Add 5cm (2in) to the length and width of the finished quilt. If the quilt is wider than the wadding, calculate the total yardage needed in the same way as for the backing.

# Preparing the fabric

Most fabric is made by weaving weft threads across taut warp threads, which run down the length of the fabric. This creates a selvedge along each long edge. The fabric gives to differing degrees if stretched in different directions. The straight grain runs down the length of the fabric and does not stretch much. The cross grain runs at right angles to the straight grain, stretching a little. The maximum amount of stretch runs on the bias, at 45 degrees to the selvedge.

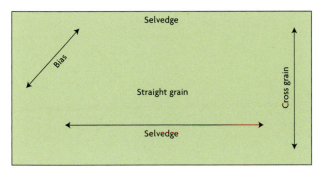

*The different grains*

## TESTING AND LAUNDERING

If you want to be able to wash your quilt, it is essential to wash the fabrics before making the quilt. This allows you to check that they are colour fast and pre-shrinks fabrics such as cotton so that it does not shrink again later. If you intend to only ever dry-clean your quilt, perhaps because the fabrics are too delicate to withstand washing, this stage is not necessary and, depending on the fabric, may not be advisable.

1 First test the fabric to make sure it is colour fast. Soak each fabric in warm water without any detergents for an hour. If the colour does bleed, soak the fabric in a solution of one part white vinegar to three parts cold water to see if you can fix the colour. If the colour still bleeds, don't use that fabric or ensure that the quilt is only ever dry-cleaned.

2 Now wash the full lengths of fabric to pre-shrink them, using a setting for a cool wash and no detergents. The fabric might have got slightly soiled anyway, but washing also removes the dressing and any loose dye.

3 When the fabric is still just slightly damp, pull it back into shape along the straight and cross grains. Then steam iron out all the creases. You could also consider starching the fabric, which gives a crisper finish suitable for rotary cutting. Hang the fabric up to dry it thoroughly.

## TRIMMING AND STORING

1 To trim the fabric, lay it out on a flat surface. Place a drafting triangle on top with one short edge along the selvedge line and the other at right angles to it. Butt a metal ruler up against the triangle and rule a line across the fabric, or use a quilter's ruler and rotary cutter on a cutting mat (see page 121). Cut across the fabric along the straight edge you have made. Then rule straight edges down both sides of the fabric and cut off the selvedges.

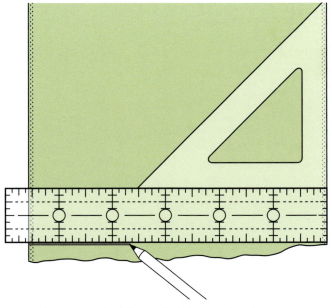

*Ruling across the fabric to find the straight edge*

2 Fold the fabrics neatly or fold and roll them. Store them somewhere clean and dry until you want to use them. If you suddenly find that you've started a collection, you could sort your fabrics into colour ranges and store them in separate transparent boxes to make them easier to select.

# Sewing skills and stitches

Whether you prefer to sew by hand or machine, you can have a completely free choice for making your quilt. Many of the most talented designers of modern quilts rely entirely on their sewing machine, while others prefer the gentle rhythm and more traditional results of hand sewing. The sewing machine will certainly save you time, but sewing by hand can be much more sociable and you can do your patchwork anywhere. Of course, you can also use both hand and machine sewing for different parts of your quilt.

You will find basic advice on sewing by hand and machine in this section. There are also instructions on how to do the stitches, including the embroidery stitches which feature in some of the projects. Advice on how to apply these skills when you are piecing patchwork, applying appliqué or quilting, is given in the section for each of those techniques. Whether you decide on hand or machine sewing, make sure that you do it in good light.

## HAND SEWING

1 Cut a 45cm (18in) length of thread. Don't be tempted to use a longer length, except for basting, because the thread is likely to tangle and wear thin. Cut the thread at an angle to aid threading the needle. Thread the freshly cut end of thread through the eye of a sharp needle. If you have difficulty threading the needle, try moistening the eye of the needle or the end of the thread to draw any splayed fibres together, or use a needle threader.

2 In order to prevent the thread from knotting and kinking, you can strengthen and stiffen it by running it over a cake of beeswax a few times. If the thread does twist, let the needle dangle on the end of it so that the thread untwists.

3 Hold the needle with a firm, but relaxed grip between your thumb and index finger, resting the eye of the needle against a thimble on your middle finger.

4 Start by securing the thread with three small backstitches, one on top of the other. Hold the fabric so that you can see the line to be stitched, including both seam lines when piecing patchwork. Aim to make stitches

of the same length, with an even tension. If the stitches are too wide apart and/or the tension is too loose, seams will gape and the fabrics may eventually fall apart. If the tension is too tight, the fabric will pucker. With practice, you will develop a steady rhythm that gives regular stitches and even tension.

5 When you reach the end point, fasten off the thread by making a back stitch knot.

## BACK STITCH KNOT

It is essential to fasten the ends of threads securely. One method for fastening off a line of stitching uses a back stitch knot. (a) Make a back stitch, bringing the needle up at the end of the stitch. (b) Pull the thread through, but leave the stitch as a small loop. (c) Take the needle through the loop of the back stitch and then through the resulting loop. (d) Pull the thread to make a knot and trim the thread.

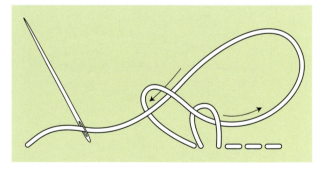

*Making a back stitch knot*

## HAND SEWING STITCHES
### Running stitch

This is the main stitch for sewing seams and for quilting. Use thread in a colour to match the fabrics, or slightly darker if necessary. Working the needle up and down through the fabric along the stitching line, make straight stitches that are about 1–2mm ($\frac{1}{16}$in) long. Pick up a few stitches on the needle at a time and then pull the thread through the fabric. The stitches should look the same on the front and the back.

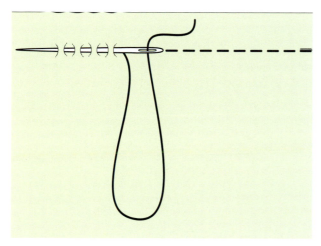

*Running stitch*

**Quilter's tip** *As you are sewing a seam, work a single back stitch every few centimetres (inch or so) to reinforce it and then return to running stitch.*

## Basting

Also called tacking, these are temporary stitches that hold pieces of fabric together until the permanent stitching is in place. Use a relatively long thread in a colour that contrasts with the fabric so that it can easily be seen. Tie a knot in the end of the thread and bring the needle up to the right side of the fabric. Pick up a few long running stitches at a time. They should be about 6mm ($\frac{1}{4}$in) long with 6mm ($\frac{1}{4}$in) spaces between each stitch.

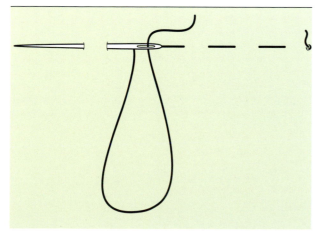

*Basting*

## Stab stitch

This stitch is used where it is too difficult to do running stitch, for example where seam allowances make the layers of fabric too unyielding. Hold the needle at right angles to the surface and take it up and down along the stitching line, making one stitch at a time.

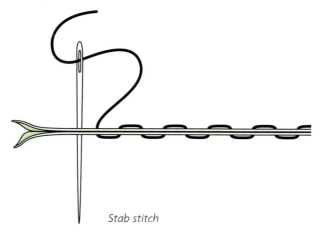

*Stab stitch*

## Back stitch

Back stitch gives a firm finish and is excellent for starting and finishing, and for seams that need to be very durable. (a) Bring the needle up on the stitching line, 3mm ($\frac{1}{8}$in) from the end. (b) Take the needle down at the start of the line, making a back stitch 3mm ($\frac{1}{8}$in) long. Bring the needle back up on the stitching line 3mm ($\frac{1}{8}$in) in front of the first stitch. (c) Continue making back stitches of the same length in this way. The stitches look continuous on the front, but overlap on the back.

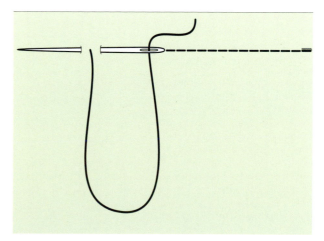

*Back stitch*

## Slip stitch

This almost invisible stitch is used for stitching down the folded edges of appliqué or bindings. (a) Bring the needle up through the fold of the top piece of fabric. (b) Insert the needle very close to where it came up, but in the background fabric. (c) Bring the needle up through the folded edge again about 3–6mm ($\frac{1}{8}$–$\frac{1}{4}$in) away. (d) Continue making evenly spaced stitches in this way.

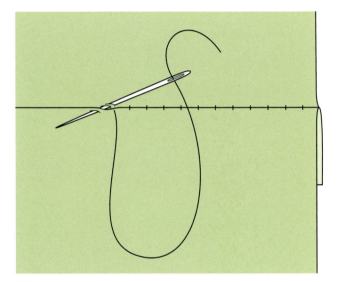

*Slip stitch*

## HAND EMBROIDERY STITCHES

### Cross stitch

Bring the needle up at A and take it down at B to make a diagonal stitch. Come up at C, directly below B and make a diagonal stitch to D, directly above A.

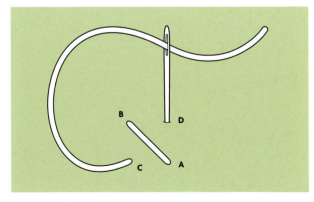

*Cross stitch*

## Fly stitch

Bring the needle up at A and take it down at B, directly to the right, but do not pull the thread right through. Come up at C, mid-way below A and B, and pull the thread through over the top of the previous stitch. Take the needle down at D, directly below C, to catch the first stitch down in a large v-shape. The proportions of your stitches may vary to give a more random effect.

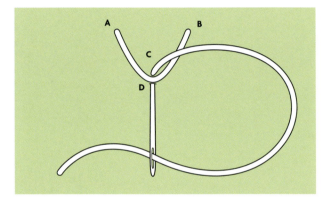

*Fly stitch*

## French knot

Bring the needle up where you want the knot to be. Firmly hold the needle and pull the thread taut with the other hand. Weave the needle so that the thread winds around it two or three times. The more times you wrap the thread, the bigger the knot. Take the needle down fractionally to one side of where it came up. Gently pull the thread through to form a knot on the surface. Secure the knot with a small back stitch on the wrong side.

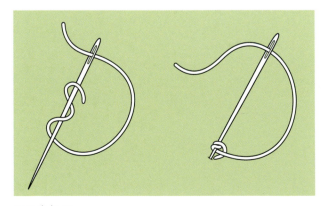

*French knot*

## Herringbone stitch

Working from left to right, bring the needle up at A. Make a diagonal stitch to B and pull the thread through. Come up at C, directly to the left of B, and make a diagonal stitch of the same length as the first down to D, directly to the right of A. Bring the needle up at E, directly to the left of D and the same distance away as from B to C. Continue in this way to make a line of stitches.

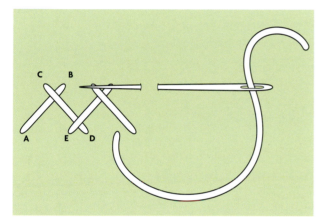

*Herringbone stitch*

## Star stitch

These isolated stars are made from a series of straight stitches. Bring the needle up at the centre of the star and make a long stitch. Repeat this so that you have eight evenly spaced stitches radiating out around the centre in a star shape.

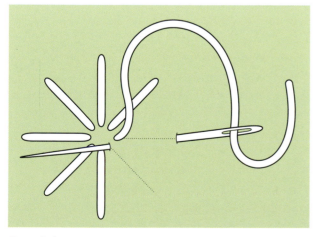

*Star stitch*

## Whipped back stitch

Make a line of back stitches and fasten off the thread. Using the same or a contrasting colour, bring the needle up underneath the first back stitch. Slip the needle below the stitch and then slip it underneath the second back stitch, from top to bottom. Continue whipping each back stitch in this way to the end of the line.

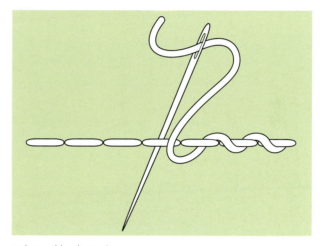

*Whipped back stitch*

## Whipped spider's web

Bring the needle up at A and down at X. Make four more evenly spaced stitches, B to E, in the same way. Bring the needle up at X, between stitches A and B. Slip the needle

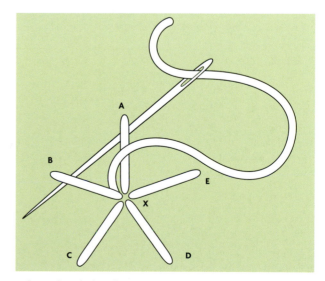

*Whipped spider's web*

under stitches A and B. Pull the thread through so that it whips over the top of stitch A. Now slip the needle under stitches B and C so that the thread whips over stitch B. Continue working in an outward spiral in this way until you have covered the base stitches.

## SETTING UP THE SEWING MACHINE

1 Follow the machine manual to thread the top and bottom threads in the sewing machine.

2 Before you start machine sewing, make sure you have an accurate gauge for your seam allowance, which will often be 6mm ($\frac{1}{4}$in). You might have a quilting foot or it might be possible to use the side edge of the presser foot as a gauge, if this is exactly the right distance from the needle.

If the foot is not the correct width, make your own gauge. Cut along one of the lines on a sheet of metric (or imperial) graph paper. Mark the line that corresponds to 6mm ($\frac{1}{4}$in) from the cut edge. Check that the needle is in the central position, put the graph paper under the machine foot and lower the needle into the paper on the marked line. Check that the paper is straight and stick a strip of masking or chiropodist's tape along the edge of the paper across the machine's throat plate.

3 Test that your gauge is accurate. Cut three 4.2 x 10cm ($1\frac{1}{2}$ x 4in) strips of scrap fabric. Sew the long sides together to make a block of three and then press the seams. Measure across the width of the middle strip, which should be exactly 3cm (1in). If it is not, adjust your gauge.

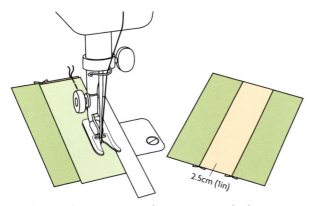

*Stitching with a seam gauge; first strip is attached; sewing second strip*

4 Always test the tension before you start sewing seams in your project pieces. Set the machine for straight stitches and the stitch length to 2 or 3. Cut two identical triangles of scrap fabric, with the long edge on the bias. Use the same weight fabric as for your quilt. Place the triangles together and sew along the bias edge. Take the fabric out of the machine, grip the ends of the seam and pull it firmly. If the needle thread breaks, the tension is too tight; if the bobbin thread breaks, the tension is too loose. Of course, you will also easily see if the one of the threads is left in loops or is puckering the fabric. Adjust the tension, following the machine manual, and then test it again.

## MACHINE SEWING

1 Slip the fabric under the presser foot, aligning the raw edge with the seam gauge. Check that the stitch length is set at 2 or 3. If your machine will sew in reverse, start by sewing a few stitches in reverse along the stitch line back to the start point. Alternatively, your machine may stitch on the spot to secure the stitches.

2 Begin sewing slowly. Place your hands on the fabric on either side just in front of the foot and spread them slightly to keep the fabric taut. Guide the fabric with your hands so that you keep sewing along the stitch line, but do not tug at it. Remove any pins before you come to them – if the needle catches pins, it will start to burr and will then snag the fabric.

3 When you reach the other end of the stitch line, sew a few reverse stitches or sew stitches on the spot to secure the thread.

4 For an alternative way to fasten off at the beginning or end of a line of stitching, first cut the threads long enough so that you can knot them together. Next pull the end of the thread which is on top gently until it pulls the bottom thread up into a loop. Put a pin through the loop and draw the bottom thread up. Thread them into a needle and take them to the wrong side. Knot the two ends together securely and trim. This method is particularly appropriate for appliqué and quilting, where the stitches start and/or finish on the quilt top and a discrete fastening is required.

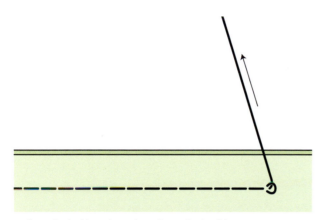

*Pulling the bobbin thread up through the fabric*

5 To work around corners and points, sew up to 2cm (³⁄₄in) from the turning point. Reset the machine to a shorter stitch and continue sewing to the turning point. Insert the needle exactly on the turning point. Lift the foot and turn the fabric. Check against the seam gauge that the new stitch line will be the correct width and adjust the position of the needle if necessary. Continue sewing small stitches for 2cm (³⁄₄in) along the next stitch line and then return to regular ones.

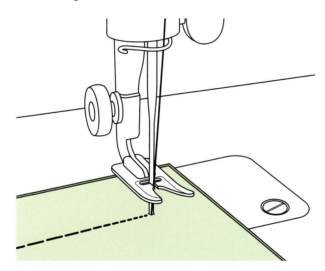

*Sewing up to a corner*

## MACHINE STITCHES

### Running stitch

Although your sewing machine might have a range of elaborate stitches which you can use for quilting, you can rely on the basic stitches most of the time. Use ordinary straight stitches, with the length set at 2 or 3, for sewing seams and for quilting. The stitches should hold the fabrics together securely, but not be too small and impossible to remove.

### Basting

You can also sew basting stitches on the sewing machine. Reset the stitch length for the longest straight stitch and don't fasten off the threads at the beginning and end.

### Close satin stitch

Use this stitch to secure the edges of appliqué shapes. Attach a zigzag, appliqué or clear plastic foot to the machine. Alter the stitch settings to a very short stitch length and a medium zigzag. Thread the machine with a colour to match the appliqué fabric. Start with the needle in the right hand position and align the edge of the appliqué so that the needle goes down fractionally to the right of it. Sew slowly and make sure that the whole width of the stitch catches the appliquéd fabric.

To sew around curves, pivot the needle by inserting it in the fabric, lifting the presser foot and rotating the fabric. Pivot with the needle in the appliquéd fabric for concave shapes, but in the background fabric for convex shapes. It is worth experimenting with this on scrap fabric first.

*Close satin stitch*

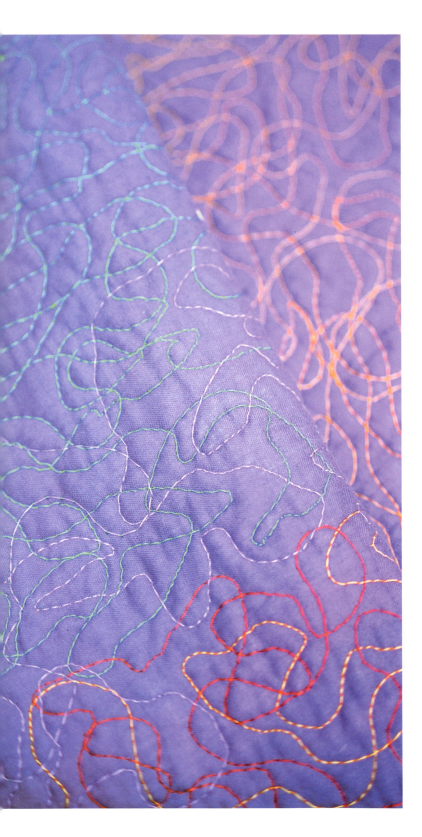

### Free-motion stitching

You need to set the machine up for free-motion stitching for meandering vermicelli stitch or free-flowing machine embroidery. Attach a darning foot if your machine requires one and set the stitch length to zero. Drop the feed dogs so that you can move the work freely in any direction. Lower the foot lever as usual to engage the thread. Draw the bobbin thread up and hold both threads when you start sewing so that they do not tangle. Keep the fabric taut with your hands or put it into an embroidery hoop. Guide the work and move the fabric smoothly to obtain small, even stitches (the length of stitch is controlled by how fast or slowly you move the fabric). Try not to work too slowly as a quicker speed will give you more even stitches.

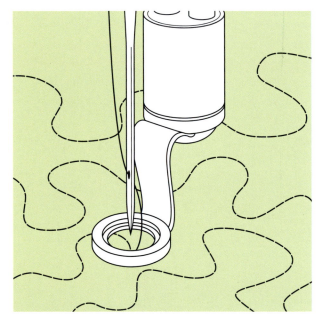

*Vermicelli stitch*

### Removing machine stitches

Don't be tempted to rip a seam apart, either with your hands or with a seam ripper, because you might tear the fabric and will definitely pull it out of shape. Using the seam ripper with care, cut the stitches at intervals. If it won't go under the stitches, ease them up with a pin before cutting them. Then turn the fabric over and pull the bottom thread. Pick off the remaining bits of thread.

# Pressing

## PRESSING GUIDELINES

You'll need your iron set up for all the stages of making your quilt because pressing is essential for a professional finish. Applying pressure to the fabric with a clean, hot steam iron will remove any deeper creases and set the seams. Apply pressure to one area at a time, lifting the iron to the next position rather than gliding it, so as not to distort the fabric.

## PRESSING SEAMS

Get into the habit of pressing each seam before you join one set of patchwork pieces to another. This makes the patchwork easier to sew together and ensures that the seams align accurately. Always press seam allowances to one side. This produces a stronger seam, preventing the wadding from working out between the stitches. Ideally, press the seam allowances towards the darker fabric, so that a shadow does not appear through the lighter fabric. It is also best to press aligning seams in opposite directions to minimize bulk. Finally, some curved seams seem to dictate which way they will lie, so press in this direction to get them to lie flat.

1 Place the pieces of fabric on the ironing board with the fabric you want to press the seam allowance towards on top. Press the seam with the right sides together to embed the stitches.

2 Then open out the top fabric and smooth it down so that

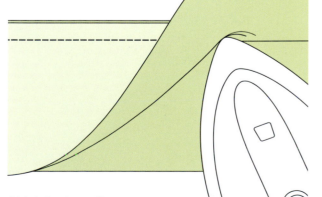

*Lightly ironing to flatten a seam*

both seam allowances stay underneath the top fabric. Lightly iron, gliding across the seam from the bottom to the top fabric, or finger press along it to temporarily flatten the seam out. To finger press, run a finger nail along the seam, firmly pushing the finger down with your thumb.

3 Place a clean pressing cloth over the seam in order to prevent the fabric from glazing. Press the seam, lifting the iron from each position, rather than gliding it across the fabric.

4 If you have had to press the seam towards the lighter fabric, carefully trim back the seam allowance on the darker fabric before you sew these pieces to others. This will minimize any dark shadow that might be visible through the lighter fabric.

## PRESSING DELICATE FABRICS

Pure cotton fabric is recommended for patchwork because it doesn't distort or fray easily and any puckers can be pressed out with a hot iron. Other fabrics may be too flimsy or silky to stay in place, fray too much, especially for appliqué, or react badly to heat. Steam is often not advisable for delicate or synthetic fabrics and threads. This doesn't mean that you can't use them, but they need treating with care and are perhaps not the best choice for a first quilt.

Always use a heat setting to suit the fabric and a pressing cloth if pressing on the right side of the fabric. Place embroidery right side down on a thick towel or fabrics with a pile such as velvet right side down on another piece of velvet. Steam press gently to avoid flattening the pile or embroidery stitches. If you are at all unsure, experiment on a similar piece of scrap fabric first.

## PRESSING APPLIQUE

Press all the pieces of cut appliqué before applying them to the fabric. When all the appliqué is stitched in place, press the design gently under a pressing cloth. Avoid over pressing as this may leave the impression of the underlying turnings on the surface.

# Patchwork

In many people's minds, the top of a patchwork quilt is synonymous with the very idea of a quilt. There are lots of different styles of quilt from which you can choose. The random shapes found in crazy patchwork are a reminder of the early days of English quilting, a technique when often tiny pieces of precious fabric were stitched together to avoid wasting them. There are hundreds of designs for the repeating block, which is such an essential part of the way patchwork developed in North America. Now quilt makers around the world still delight in these traditions, but many also design complicated geometric or free-flowing patchworks. They can all be works of art, just with very different characters.

The success of a patchwork quilt top lies in accuracy, as well as the more obvious design features – accurate measuring tools and templates, cutting of fabric and sewing of seams.

## MAKING TEMPLATES

Templates are firm patterns which are marked around to transfer the outline of a shape onto the fabric. They are conventionally given in two ways – templates with and without a seam allowance included. Patchwork templates often give a seam allowance, but appliqué and quilting templates do not.

The seam allowance that is often given for patchwork and appliqué is 6mm ($\frac{1}{4}$in) and this is the allowance most often for the quilts found in this book. However, you will also see the term 'scant $\frac{1}{4}$in' used, which means two threads of the fabric less than $\frac{1}{4}$in and equates to about 5mm.

None of the quilts in this book require patchwork templates. Instead, all the necessary pieces are cut out with a quicker method, using a rotary cutter (see pages 120–22). However, if you do need to make patchwork templates, use the following method.

1 Identify the appropriate templates for your project and trace them out or enlarge them if necessary, according to the accompanying instructions.

2 Choose a suitable material from which to make your templates. If you are using card, spray glue the tracing onto the card. Alternatively, place template plastic over the top of the tracing and trace the shapes onto the plastic.

3 Carefully cut round the edges of the template with paper scissors. It is important that the templates are absolutely accurate, so check them by placing each one over the original.

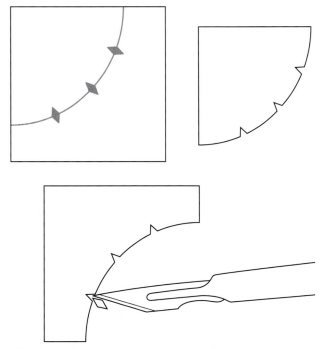

*Marking and cutting out registration marks on curved edges*

4 If any of the templates have curved edges or other shapes that will be hard to replicate it is a good idea to make registration marks on the seams of neighbouring templates before cutting them apart. Cut the registration marks out or mark them with a permanent marker.

5 Label each template with the name of the pattern piece, any grain line and the number to cut. Also mark if it is to be cut in reverse.

## MARKING OUT THE FABRIC

You will need to use templates to mark out the more complex patchwork shapes onto the fabric. You can also use a template to mark out simple geometric shapes, but it is much quicker and easier to cut these shapes and straight strips out in batches using a rotary cutter and quilter's ruler, and you will find instructions for doing this on pages 120–22. However you decide to cut your patchwork pieces out, remember to use a template the exact size of the finished shape for hand sewing, marking the seam allowance on the fabric, and a template that includes the seam allowances for machine sewing.

1 Prepare a flat surface for marking out the fabric. It helps if the surface is not too shiny so that the fabric does not slip, so use a large cutting mat or cover a table with a smoothed-out sheet.

2 First, consider whether you need to take the nap, grain line or pattern on the fabric into account before marking and cutting the shapes. For example, you may want the pattern to run in the same direction down the quilt, along or across the various borders and sashes. Equally, you may want a particular motif to appear on each piece of patchwork. It is also important to cut fabrics with any pile or directional sheen in the right direction. If so, you will need to mark out the pieces accordingly.

3 Place the fabric on the flat surface, right side down. Make sure that the edges of the fabric are straight (see page 109).

4 Using a water-soluable marker or a quilter's pencil, mark out the patchwork pieces on the fabric. If you are going to sew the pieces together by machine, make sure that the template you use to mark out your shapes includes a 6mm (¼in) seam allowance. Mark out the total number of pieces you need of each shape together, so that they fit snugly with the least amount of wastage and can be cut out along the minimum number of lines. Place the template right side down on the reverse of the fabric, aligning the grain arrow with the straight or cross grain of the fabric. If there is no grain arrow, position one of the straight edges of each shape on the straight or cross grain and any curved edges on the bias. If you need to reverse any shapes, position them, wrong side down, on the reverse of the fabric.

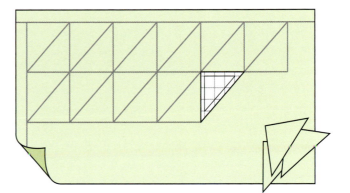

*Marking out rows of triangles on the wrong side of the fabric, ready for machine sewing*

5 If you are going to sew the patchwork by hand, use a template that does not include the seam allowance. Align the template with the grain as necessary. When you position the template on the fabric, allow enough space between each outline for the seam allowances of both shapes. Fit the shapes close together as for machine sewing. Then mark a dot at each end of each seam.

Then add the 6mm (¼in) seam allowance. A quick way to add it is to use a quilter's quarter or a quarter wheel, depending on whether you are dealing with straight or curved edges. Align the edge of the quilter's quarter with the seam line and mark the cutting line on the opposite side. Position the next shape another seam allowance away from the previous one and mark that out too. Remember to cut around the outer lines.

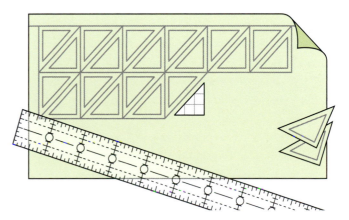

*Marking out rows of triangles and adding the seam allowances, ready for hand sewing*

## CUTTING OUT PATCHWORK PIECES

It's a good idea to cut out all the pieces you need for the quilt top at the same time. That way you can be sure that you have all the fabric you need and it saves time, especially if you cut the pieces in batches. Sort them by shape and colour, and pop each set into a plastic bag with a note to identify their position on the design. This keeps them clean and you'll also be able to find the pieces you want easily.

### Cutting individual shapes

When you have marked out all the shapes on the fabrics, cut them out with either dressmaker's scissors or a rotary cutter. A cutter is ideal for cutting shapes with straight lines quickly and easily, but scissors are better for appliqué pieces and other shapes with curved lines. Before you start, check that you have marked out all the necessary seam allowances.

### Quick cutting with dressmaker's scissors

This technique speeds up the process of cutting out strips and simple geometric shapes such as squares, rectangles and triangles. You can cut up to six layers of fabric without having to mark out all the shapes first.

1 Carefully count the number of each different shape you need to cut from each fabric. Then work out how many layers of fabric you need to work with. For example, you might be able to cut 12 triangles from the width of the fabric. If you need 36 triangles in one fabric, you can cut the fabric to half width and work with six layers. The idea is to cut out as many shapes together as possible to save time.

2 Place one piece of fabric right side down on a flat surface. Working from the straight, cross-grain edge, mark out one strip of shapes across the width. Now layer the other pieces of fabric right sides down on a protected, flat surface. Align the straight edges and press each layer of fabric as it goes down, finishing with the marked fabric on top.

3 Pin through all the layers of fabric inside the cutting lines of every shape, so that the pins do not need to be removed for cutting. First cut along the longest lines to make strips. Then cut the individual shapes.

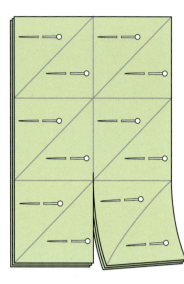

*Cutting triangles with dressmaker's scissors*

4 To cut out some of the shapes in reverse, arrange the appropriate number of layers of fabric in pairs with right sides together. If you are using a template to mark out the fabric, use it the right way round, not reversed. The fabric that is wrong side up will produce reverse shapes.

### Quick cutting with a rotary cutter

Using a rotary cutter is the quickest way to cut batches of simple geometric shapes. Make sure that the blade is sharp and that you work on a cutting mat.

If you are left-handed, you may find it best to work with the rotary ruler and cutter on the opposite sides to those shown in the illustrations.

1 Fold the fabric in half along the straight grain, aligning the long edges. Press the fabric, especially along the fold. Repeat the process so that you have four layers of fabric.

2 Place the folded fabric on the cutting mat. Position a rotary ruler a short way from the short end of the fabric. Check that it is at right angles to the fold by aligning the short lines across the ruler with the fold. Arching your left hand and keeping your fingers well away from the edge, press firmly down on the ruler. Starting at the end closest to you, run the rotary cutter away from you

along the right-hand side of the ruler in a smooth, steady movement. Stop cutting just after you pass your left hand and, keeping the cutter in place, move the left hand further along the ruler. Continue in this way until you have trimmed off the end of the fabric.

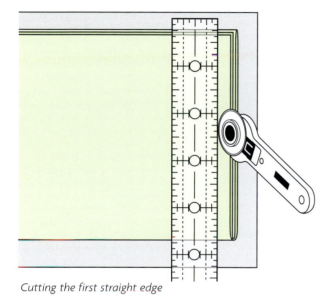

*Cutting the first straight edge*

3 Now rotate the cutting mat, so that you are ready to cut the fabric into strips from left to right. Decide on the width of strip that you need, remembering to add

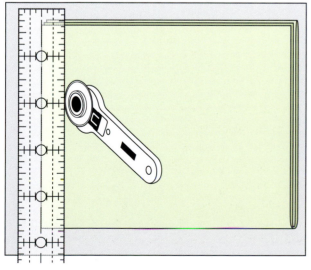

*Cutting the first strip*

seam allowances, and align the vertical line on the ruler that gives the correct strip width along the left-hand edge of the fabric. Press down on the ruler, holding the first strip firm, and run the cutter along the right-hand side of the ruler in the same way as before.

4 Open out the first strip and check that it is perfectly straight. Repeat the process to cut the required number of strips.

5 Press the strips in the appropriate number of layers, remembering that some may need to be right sides together to create reverse shapes. Return the fabric to the cutting mat and you can then cut a variety of different shapes from the strips.

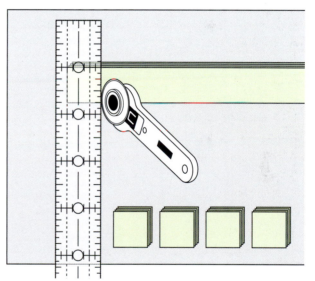

*Cutting strips into squares*

**Quilter's tip** *Always run the rotary cutter away from, never towards you, and remember to retract the blade when you have finished using the cutter.*

### Squares or rectangles

Place the strips of fabric across the cutting mat from your left to right. With the quilter's ruler at right angles to the fabric, trim off the short edge as before. Rotate the mat and align the ruler to give the correct length of the square or rectangle, remembering to add the seam allowances. Cut the shape and repeat the process to make the required number.

### Half-square triangles

Cut these right-angled triangles from squares. The short sides of the finished triangles are on the straight or cross grain and the long side is on the bias.

1 Cut the preliminary squares so that the finished length of the sides is the same as the finished length of the short sides of the triangles. Most designs specify the measurements of the pieces you need. However, if you are designing your own, you will need to add more than the usual 6mm ($\frac{1}{4}$in) seam allowance to each side to allow for the points on the triangle. The 'magic number' to allow for the seam allowances of half-square triangles is 2.1cm ($\frac{7}{8}$in). Add this to the finished length of the short sides.

2 Cut one diagonal line across each square, holding the quilter's ruler down firmly to ensure that the corners are cut accurately.

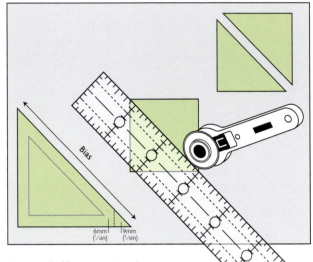

*Cutting half-square triangles*

### Quarter-square triangles

You can also cut these triangles from squares. The long side of the triangle is on the straight or cross grain and the short sides are on the bias.

1 Cut the preliminary squares so that the finished length of the sides is the same as the finished length of the long sides of the triangles. The 'magic number' to add to the finished length of the long side is 3cm (1 $\frac{1}{4}$in).

2 Cut one diagonal across each square and then cut each half-square triangle in half again to make a total of four quarter-square triangles.

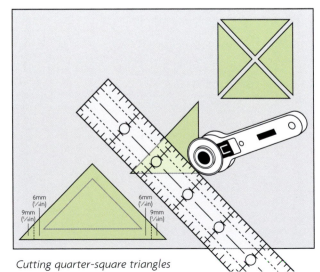

*Cutting quarter-square triangles*

## PIECING PATCHWORK

By marking and cutting the fabric shapes accurately, you are half way to perfect patchwork. However, piecing the patchwork together with the greatest precision is equally important. It isn't difficult if you follow a few basic principles and make sure that you pay close attention to the detail.

Whether you want to sew by hand or machine, try to follow a basic sequence that minimizes the number of times you need to stop and start or have to piece awkward shapes together. As a general rule, sew together the smallest pieces first and then join them up to make rows. Then sew the rows together to make blocks. Finally, sew the blocks together into units before adding the sashes and borders.

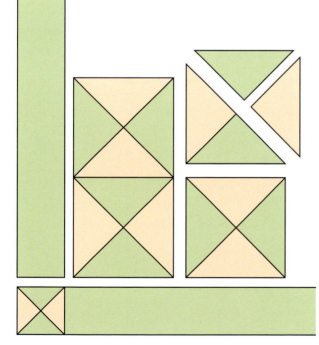

*An efficient sequence for piecing patchwork*

### Piecing by hand

Patchwork was originally pieced together by hand and many people still prefer to do it that way. The work is portable, so you can sew with friends or on a journey, or just move into better light. Hand piecing also gives a beginner more control over matching the seams.

### Straight seams

1 With the seam lines marked on the wrong side of the fabric, match the edges of two adjacent shapes. Insert a pin through both layers of fabric exactly through the dot on one corner, at right angles to the seam. Secure the pin inside the seam allowance. Pin the other corner in the same way. Add at least one more pin at the centre of the seam line and others if necessary for a long seam.

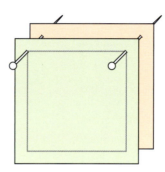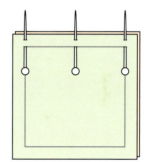

2 Thread a sharp needle and, removing the first pin, secure the thread with three small back stitches at the corner point. Sew small running stitches along the seam line, checking the accuracy on the back from time to time and removing the pins before you reach

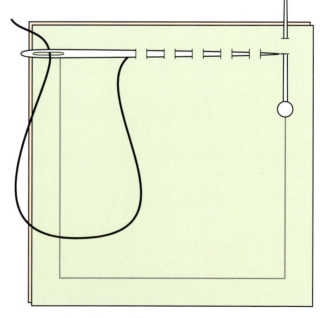

*Sewing along the seam line*

them. Secure the thread at the next corner with a back stitch knot (see page 110) or three small back stitches. Sew right up to the end of the seam line, but never sew into the seam allowance.

**Quilter's tip** *Every few centimetres (inch or so), make a single back stitch to reinforce a seam.*

3 Press the seam allowance towards the darker fabric or to ensure that adjoining seams lie in opposite directions (see page 117), before joining these shapes to others to make up a row.

4 To join rows of patchwork pieces, place two rows right sides together and align the long edges. First, pin through the corners at each end of the row. Then insert pins through the existing seam lines, to match those that will butt up to each other. Keeping the seam allowances loose, insert two more pins on each side of each existing seam. Finally, pin along the rest of the seam line as necessary.

5 Secure the thread at the first corner as before and sew a running stitch along the new seam line, removing the pins as you reach them. Sew right up to existing seams, keeping the seam allowance loose, and secure the thread with a back stitch. Take the needle through the existing seam allowance close to the seam and secure the thread with a back stitch again on the other side. Continue sewing along the seam line and secure the thread at the end.

### Joining quarter-square triangles

1 Align two of the short edges of two triangles and sew them together to make a larger triangle. Fasten off the thread with a back stitch at the end of the seam line. Open out the triangles and press the seam allowance

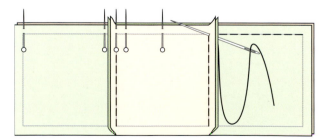

*Sewing two rows of squares together*

towards the darker fabric. Repeat the process on another pair of triangles, pressing the seam allowance to the opposite side.

2 Align the long edges of the two new triangles and pin them together through the outer corners. Then insert pins through the existing seam lines, which will butt up to each other. Keeping the seam allowances loose, insert two more pins on each side of the existing seams. Finally, pin along the rest of the new seam line as necessary.

3 Sew along the new seam line up to the existing seams, keeping the seam allowance loose, and secure the thread with a back stitch. Take the needle through the existing seam allowance close to the seam and secure the thread again on the other side. Continue sewing along the seam line and secure the thread at the end.

4 Open the square out and press the new seam allowance to one side. These pieced squares can be sewn into strips to make a patchwork border or incorporated into more complex blocks.

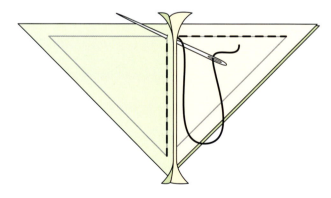

*Sewing two pairs of triangles together*

### Curved seams

1 Sewing curved seams so that the fabrics lie flat when opened out can seem difficult, with too much fabric on the concave curve and too little on the convex one. To make it easier, transfer the registration marks on the templates to the wrong side of the fabric pieces. There should be at least three – at the midpoint on the seam and at a point on each side of the centre, half way towards each end of the seam. You may need more marks along tighter curves.

2 Pin the seams together, matching the marks and both ends of the seam. Ease the edge of the concave piece of fabric to align with the edge of the convex piece, or vice versa, as you find easiest. Pin along the seam to align the lines perfectly. You can also clip into the seam allowance on the curved edges if this helps to ease the fabric into shape, but this is usually only necessary on very tight curves.

3 Carefully, sew along the seam line as usual to join the shapes, checking the accuracy on the back from time to time. Press the seam allowance towards the convex shape.

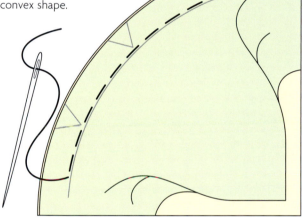

*Sewing curved shapes together*

### Piecing by machine

Piecing patchwork with a sewing machine is much quicker than sewing by hand. It is extremely popular and gives seams a more distinct edge. However, of course you are tied to the sewing machine.

### Straight seams

1 Shapes for machine piecing are cut out without the seam lines being marked, so you must be confident about using a seam gauge to sew an accurate seam (see page 114).

2 Align the adjacent edges of two fabric shapes and pin the seams together as for hand piecing.

3 Secure the thread with a few back stitches (see page 114) and sew slowly along the seam, removing the pins just before you get to them. Press the seam allowance to one side, before joining pieces together to make a row.

4 When you have lots of fabric pieces to pair together, save time and thread by piecing batches of the same shape together in a long chain. Sew the seam on the first pair of fabric pieces. Without sewing any securing stitches, lifting the presser foot or cutting the thread, gently pull the threads out a little and feed the next pair of shapes through the machine. Continue in this way until all the pairs are sewn together in a chain. Then, cut the threads between the pieces and press all the seam allowances to one side.

*Chain piecing triangles together*

5 To join rows, first make sure that the seam allowances that will align with each other are pressed in opposite directions to reduce bulk. Place two rows right sides together and align the long edges. Insert pins through the corners at each end of the row. Then pin together the existing seam lines, to match those that will butt up to each other. Insert two more pins on each side of each existing seam, securing the seam allowance. Finally, pin along the rest of the seam line as necessary.

6 Secure the thread at the first corner as before and slowly sew along the new seam line, right across the existing seams and allowances. Remove the pins as you reach them and secure the thread at the other end of the new seam line.

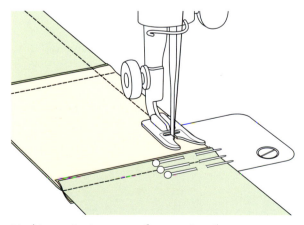

*Machine sewing two rows of squares together*

### Curved seams

1 Use the same methods of pinning together, matching registration marks and easing the two edges into alignment as for hand piecing (see page 125). Clip into the seam allowance on the curved edges if this helps to ease the fabric into shape.

2 Secure the thread at the beginning of the seam line and slowly sew along the seam, taking care to follow the seam gauge all the way round. Also take care to keep the fabric eased evenly round the seam and that the presser foot does not push the excess fabric forward. You might need to experiment to find out whether your machine handles the excess fabric best if it is on top or on the bottom. Do not tug at the fabric because when the curve is cut on the bias, it will be more prone to pulling out of shape than usual. Press the seam allowance towards the convex shape.

### Attaching borders

When all the patchwork or appliqué is complete, long strips of fabric can be attached around the edges to make borders. They can be mitred at the corners or the top and bottom borders can be attached straight across the side borders. Before cutting the fabric for the borders, check the size of the main quilt top because it might have come up slightly differently to expectation. Put a pin at the midpoint along each edge and measure across the middle of the quilt from pin to opposite pin. This gives you the most accurate measurements for the side and top and bottom borders because the edges of the quilt top may have become distorted. Then you need to add a further allowance depending on whether you want straight or mitred corners (see the relevant sections below). If the edges of the quilt top are a slightly different measurement, you will need to ease them to fit the borders. Only trim them if this is not detrimental to the design and/or ease the edges to fit.

### Straight-cornered borders

1 Cut two side borders to the width specified in the project and the same length as the quilt top, plus seam allowances all round. Fold each border in half, matching short ends together, and press.

2 Cut the other two borders to the same width, but as long as the short edges of the quilt top, adding twice the border width and seam allowances. Fold and press the borders as before.

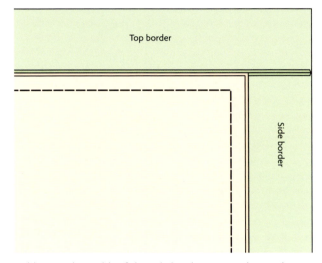

*Add twice the width of the side border to give the total length of the top border*

3 Match the centre fold on one of the side borders to the corresponding pin on the quilt top and pin them right sides together. Align the raw edges and baste the seam. Sew the border to the quilt top either by hand or on the sewing machine. Attach the opposite border in the same way. Press the seam allowances towards the borders.

4 Pin the bottom border across the bottom edges of the quilt top and both side borders. Baste and then sew it in position. Repeat the process on the top border. Press the seam allowances towards the new borders.

### Mitred borders

1 Calculate the length of the side borders by adding twice the width of the border plus seam allowances to the length of the quilt top. Calculate the length of the other two borders in the same way, based on the width of the quilt top.

2 Pin the long borders in place in the same way as for straight-cornered borders. Sew the seams exactly to the points at the corners where the borders meet but no further. Attach the top and bottom borders in the same way. Press the seam allowances towards the borders.

3 To mitre a corner by hand, lay the quilt top right side up on a flat surface with the side border smoothed out underneath the adjoining border. Using a water-erasable marker or a quilter's pencil, mark a line from the inner corner of the border to the point where the outer edges of the two strips of fabric cross each other. Fold the top border under along the line and pin it on top of the side border. Using matching thread, slip stitch the mitre in place (see page 112). Press the corner and repeat the process to mitre the other three.

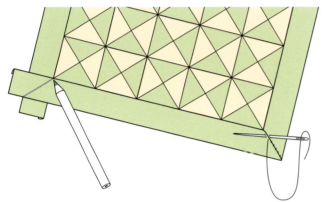

*Marking and sewing the seams for a mitred border*

To mitre a corner on the sewing machine, work on the wrong side. Lay the quilt top right side down on a flat surface with the side border smoothed out underneath the adjoining border. Mark the mitre line in the same way as for mitring by hand. Then place the bottom border on top and mark another line in the same way. Align the two seam lines and pin them, right sides together. Machine sew along the line. Trim the seam allowances and press the seam open. Repeat the process to mitre the other corners.

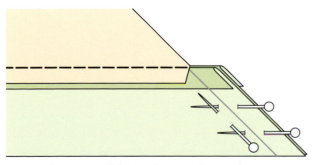

*Pinning the corners of the borders together, ready to mitre the seam*

# Appliqué

The dramatic effect of an appliqué design can add great vibrancy to a quilt. Traditional designs were usually inspired by familiar objects in nature and the home environment, and this desire to incorporate images of personal significance continues in modern quilts.

There are several ways of applying the appliqué pieces by both hand and machine, so you can choose the method that best suits you and the design. The Liberty's Song Bird quilt uses hand methods, whereas Gumleaves takes advantage of the machine for reverse appliqué. Working by hand is slower, but in the first instance gives you greater control over the shapes and their placement. The sewing machine offers a quicker method and the possibility of different effects.

## PATTERNS AND TEMPLATES

A template is needed for each different shape in an appliqué design. You can trace the template outlines for the appliqué quilts in this book from the section at the back. Most are given at full size, although you will need to scale larger shapes up to full size. All the appliqué outlines are given without turning allowances.

Full-scale design patterns are useful for giving you the precise placement of all the appliqué pieces, as well as for producing large templates. Precise positioning of the pieces can be especially important in a design that demands symmetry or a regular repeat. If there is just one overall design and you are feeling confident, you could position the pieces by eye instead. Scale up a full-size pattern from the book by using a grid.

## ENLARGING A PATTERN BY GRID

1 Tape a piece of tracing paper over the design and trace the pattern, including the outline. Draw a rectangle around the pattern if one is not already provided. Mark off regular intervals along all four edges of the rectangle. Then join aligning marks to make a grid over the pattern. The more detailed the pattern, the closer the grid lines need to be.

2 Now place a sheet of paper large enough to take the full-size pattern on a flat surface. Measure out an outline for the full-size pattern in the same proportions as the rectangle around the pattern, using a drafting triangle and metal ruler to make sure that the corners are square. Mark off the same number of regular intervals along the edges of this new outline as for the first grid. Join the marks to make a grid as before.

3 Whilst constantly referring to the traced pattern, draw out the shapes from the original to the enlarged pattern one square at a time. When you have finished doing this, adjust any lines on the enlargement that are not smooth or accurate. Finally, go over the design lines with a permanent marker.

*Copying a design from a small grid to a larger one*

4 Label each pattern piece with a name and a number, according to the layering sequence on the background fabric. Also add the grain lines.

5 Trace the templates for each appliqué shape onto tracing paper from your full-size pattern, adding a lapping allowance on shapes that lie underneath others.

## Making appliqué templates

1 Durable templates, for making multiples of the same shapes, can be made out of thin card or template plastic. If you are going to use card, first trace the outlines for the templates onto tracing or greaseproof (waxed) paper. Then spray-glue the tracing onto the card. Alternatively, place template plastic over the template outlines and trace the shapes onto the plastic.

2 Cut the templates out with scissors or put them onto a cutting mat and carefully cut round the edges using a craft knife. The templates must be absolutely accurate, so check them by placing each one over the original outline.

3 Not all templates need to be as durable as card or plastic ones. Sometimes you will only need to use each template once or a few times. Trace the outlines for these templates straight onto greaseproof (waxed) or the shiny side of freezer paper.

## PREPARING THE FABRICS

If the appliquéd element of your quilt is quite simple or one large design, you might not need to mark it out on the background fabric. However, if the appliqué is repeated in the same place on lots of blocks or the design is complex or perfectly symmetrical, marking the fabric first will improve the finished results. It is also important to plan the order of positioning the appliqué shapes on complex designs, especially if you are going to fuse the fabrics together.

1 Cut the background fabric to size, adding a 1cm (½in) allowance all round in addition to the seam allowance, to cater for any take up of fabric during the appliqué process. Iron the fabric flat.

2 Fold the fabric in half across the width and then the length. Gently press the folds into place to find the midpoint of the piece of fabric.

3 Trace the design pattern onto the fabric as a guide if you wish.

## Tracing the design

1 Centre the background fabric over the pattern, both right sides up, and pin them together. Place them over a light source. This could be a light box or you could tape them to a large window or glass-topped table with a lamp underneath.

2 Using a quilter's pencil in a colour that will show up, trace the pattern onto the right side of the fabric, marginally inside the outline of each shape, just to give a positional guide.

## Making appliqué shapes

The shapes for hand and machine appliqué can be marked, cut and applied in various ways, depending on the sewing technique, the quilting design and personal preference.

## Using templates for hand appliqué

This basic technique is suitable for making lots of shapes from the same template ready for hand appliqué. Remember that these shapes will need a scant 6mm (¼in) turning allowance.

1 Place the fabric right side up on a flat surface. Position the template right side up on the fabric, matching the grain line and with enough space for the turning allowance all round.

2 Mark around the template with a sharp pencil. Mark out the whole shape, even if another fabric in the design will be placed over the top of it. Mark out all the shapes needed in that fabric, allowing for the turnings on

*Marking out a series of shapes for appliqué*

each one. If reverse shapes are needed, place the template right side down before marking round it.

3 Cut out the shapes round the outline for the turning allowance, ready to hand stitch them to the background fabric.

### Using freezer paper

This method will stabilize flimsy and lightweight fabrics or give a crisp outline to hand appliquéd shapes. The paper is taken out before the stitching is completed.

1 Trace the template outline directly from the original onto the shiny side of the freezer paper. Then cut around the shape.

2 Place the fabric right side down on a flat surface. Press the freezer paper, shiny side down, onto the wrong side of the fabric. Cut around the shape, adding the allowance.

3 When you apply the shape to the background fabric, slip stitch around most of the edge. Then remove the freezer paper, before completing the stitching.

### Using interfacing

Interfacing will also stabilize fabric and give a crisp outline to hand appliquéd shapes. However, it does increase the bulk of the fabric and can make quilting across the shapes less easy.

1 Lay a piece of lightweight iron-on interfacing, non-adhesive side up, on a flat surface. Place the template, right side down, on the interfacing. Using a pencil, mark round the edges of the template. Mark out all the shapes you wish to cut from the same piece of fabric close together, making sure that all the grain lines align and leaving enough space for the turning allowance all round each one. Roughly cut around the whole area.

2 Place the fabric right side down on the ironing board. Position the piece of interfacing, adhesive side down, on top, aligning the grain lines. Following the manufacturer's instructions, bond the interfacing to the fabric.

3 If you feel the fabric will be difficult to manipulate, use thread that contrasts with the colour of the fabric to sew a row of running stitches (stay stitches) just inside the outline of the appliqué shape. Cut out the shapes, remembering to add the turning allowance.

### Using templates for machine appliqué

Remember that shapes for machine appliqué do not need a turning allowance.

1 Place the fabric right side up on a flat surface. Position the template right side up on the fabric, matching the grain line. If reverse shapes are needed, place the template right side down before marking round it.

2 Using a sharp pencil, mark around the template to give as many shapes as are needed, keeping them together. Mark out the whole shape, even if another fabric in the design will be placed over the top of it.

3 Cut the shapes out accurately around the outlines and then put them to one side ready to machine stitch them to the background fabric.

### Using fusible web

Paper-backed fusible web offers a quick way to cut out and apply machine appliquéd shapes. The shapes don't even need to be sewn down as the web permanently fuses them to the background fabric and will withstand machine washing. However, this technique is not ideal if you want to quilt over the appliqué design because the fabrics are fused together and the bulk cannot be cut away to reduce it. You must also remember that the image will reverse.

*Cut between the fused shapes before cutting carefully around the edges*

1 Lay the fusible web, paper side up, on a flat surface. Next place the template, right side down, on the fusible web. Then using a pencil, mark a dark line round the edges of the template. Mark out all the shapes you wish to cut from the same piece of fabric making sure they fit closely together, also make sure that all the grain lines align too. Roughly cut around each area to be fused to a different fabric with paper scissors.

2 Following the manufacturer's instructions and aligning the grain lines, fuse the fusible web to the wrong side of the fabric. Roughly cut between the fused shapes with paper scissors (see page 130) and, without removing the paper backing, put them safely to one side until you are ready to apply them to the background fabric.

### Making curved lines

You can make long, curved appliqué shapes, for example for flower stems, using a curved template, but these can be fiddly to sew in place. Instead, cut a piece of fabric on the bias, making sure that it is the correct width for the shape plus turning allowances. Also add a little extra to the length. Press the allowances under along both long sides of the strip. Curve the fabric strip along the design line on the background fabric. Baste and pin it in place, before stitching it down.

### APPLYING APPLIQUE

The decision as to whether to apply appliqué by hand or machine will have quite a distinctive impact on the finished look of your quilt. Hand stitches give a softer, more antique feel, while machine stitches are much more obvious and look more modern.

### Appliqué by hand

1 Cut the appliqué shapes out of the fabric, remembering to include a turning allowance. (Felt and other non-fraying fabrics can be cut to the finished size and slip stitched in place without a turning.) You can either mark the allowance before you make the cuts or cut by eye if you are confident of your judgement. Clip just up to the stitch line around any curves and into any valleys at right angles to the turning allowance.

*Clipping around a curved shape*

2 Using thread in a contrasting colour, baste the turning allowance. Working with the right side of the fabric facing you, turn the allowance along the outline to the wrong side of the fabric and baste it in position all round the shape. Make sure that the lines of any curves are smooth. Press the edges of the shapes very lightly, so that you do not embed an impression of the stitches on the fabric.

3 Place the background fabric on a flat surface right side up and pin all the shapes in position, taking care to overlap adjacent shapes in the correct sequence.

4 Before you begin to baste the shapes in position, you might find it helpful to stretch the design area in a large embroidery hoop to keep the background fabric taut. Only use a hoop at this stage if the whole design area fits within the hoop, otherwise there is a risk of dislodging the pinned shapes. Using a contrasting colour of thread, baste around all the edges of the shapes, removing the pins as you go. Alternatively, you could glue the shapes with a glue stick.

5 Now that the shapes are firmly basted in position, you could continue with the work in an embroidery hoop. Thread a sharp needle with a colour to match one of the

*Pinning, basting and slip stitching appliqué shapes in place*

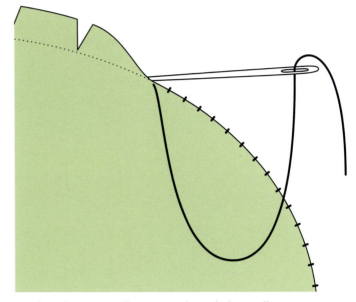

*Stroking the turning allowance under with the needle*

appliqué fabrics and knot the end. Bring the needle up from beneath the background fabric and slip stitch around the first shape (see page 112). Keep the tension firm, but not tight. Changing the colour of thread to match the fabric, slip stitch around each shape, including around the edges that overlap adjacent shapes, until they are all secure.

**Quilter's tip** *Many quilters bind the inner ring of a quilting hoop with bias binding to achieve an even better grip.*

Alternatively, you could use the quicker, but slightly less accurate method of sewing the appliqué shapes directly to the background fabric without basting. First pin the shapes in position on the background fabric. Bring the thread up to the right side and roll the turning allowance under with your finger and thumb just before you make each slip stitch around the outline. On curves and other difficult shapes, use the point of the needle to stroke, or needleturn, the turning allowance under. When all the appliqué shapes are in place, remove any basting stitches and lightly press the work on the wrong side.

6 If you wish to quilt across the appliqué design, you will need to remove any excess layers of fabric from the wrong side. This makes the fabric shape puff up a little and

also reduces the possibilities of the fabrics puckering or of a dark background showing through a lighter top fabric. However, it also has the tendency destabilize an appliqué design with large shapes.

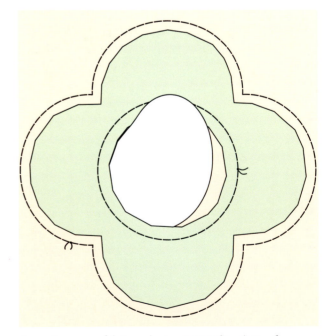

*Removing excess fabric and a temporary foundation from the wrong side*

Turn the work over to the wrong side. Pinch the background fabric within the slip stitch outlines to pull it away from the appliqué fabric and very carefully make a small cut in the background fabric. Ensuring that you cut through just one layer, cut away the background fabric to within a scant 6mm (¼in) inside the seam line.

7 Cut away any other layers of appliqué fabric that lie beneath the top layer in the same way, always checking that you are not cutting through the top layer on right side of the quilt.

## Outside corners

On corners that point outwards, excess fabric needs to be turned under discretely or cut away to reduce bulk. On a wide corner, turn one edge under and press the fold in place by running your fingers along it. Then turn under the edge on the other side of the corner, on top of the first turning. As you slip stitch the shape in place, stroke the bottom seam allowance away from the adjacent edge at the corner with the tip of your needle.

For a narrow corner, sew a line of running stitches just outside the design outline. Trim off half the point across the corner. Fold the remaining allowance under across the corner. Then fold under the side edges along the design outlines. Finally trim away the excess turning allowance (see below).

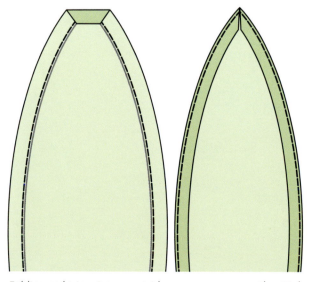

*Folding and trimming an outside corner over across the stitch line and then turning the remaining turning allowances under*

## Inside corners

On corners that point inwards, the turning allowance has to be allowed to splay open so that it will lie flat. Sew a line of stay stitches just inside the design outline. Clip across the turning allowance close to the stitching and fold the edges under. When you slip stitch the shape in place, work a few close stitches right on the corner to secure the tiny area of raw edge.

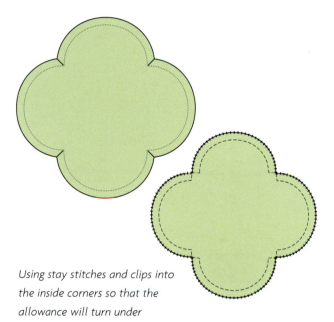

*Using stay stitches and clips into the inside corners so that the allowance will turn under*

## Machine appliqué

1 Attach a zigzag, appliqué or clear plastic foot to the sewing machine. Alter the stitch settings for close satin stitch (see page 115); use a narrower stitch for lightweight fabric and a wider stitch for heavier ones. Thread the machine with a colour to match the appliqué fabric.

2 Place the appliqué shapes on the background fabric according to the design, making sure that the shapes overlap each other in the correct way. Pin or glue the shapes in position with water-soluble adhesive.

3 Put the work into the machine and slowly sew a line of straight stitches close to the edge around each shape, taking care that the fabric does not pucker. If the fabric is too difficult to manage in this way, cut the shapes out with a 6mm (¼in) allowance, baste them in position and then trim the shape to the stitch line.

4 Now work slowly around each shape with close satin stitch, guiding the shape round without stopping to get a smooth line. Do not secure the threads on the machine at the beginning or end. Instead, leave the threads long and secure them later.

5 Pivot the work often to follow the edges accurately by inserting the needle into the fabric, lifting the sewing machine foot and turning the background fabric. This will help you to negotiate around corners and keep the stitches evenly spaced around them. For outside corners, pivot on the background fabric side and for inside corners, pivot on the appliqué side.

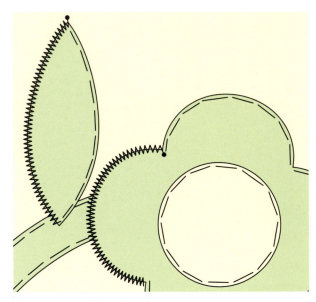

*Pivoting on outside and inside corners*

6 On tight inside curves, reduce the width of the stitch so that it tapers going into and coming out of the corner. This may not suit fabrics of heavier weight, which need a wider stitch to secure them.

7 After you have finished machining, pull each pair of threads to the wrong side, thread them into a needle and secure them with a few small back stitches without going through to the right side of the fabric.

8 Remove any basting stitches. Cut away excess layers of fabric to reduce the bulk of it from the wrong side as for hand appliqué (see pages 132–3). Finally, lightly press the appliquéd design.

## Using fusible web

1 Make sure that you know exactly where the appliqué shapes go on the background fabric and the sequence in which they must be applied. Number the shapes in the correct sequence if this will assist you.

2 Peel the backing paper off one set of shapes at a time. Cut around the outline of each shape as marked on the fusible web and place the shape on the background fabric. Then following the manufacturer's instructions, fuse each shape in position.

3 Alternatively, if the design comprises lots of shapes, fuse them together first, using a non-stick sheet or baking parchment to protect the ironing board. Then fuse the whole design to the background fabric.

4 Fused designs do not need to be stitched to the background. However, if you wish, machine sew close satin stitch (see page 115) or buttonhole stitch for a naïve style around the edges.

# Quilting

The art of quilting the top quilt, wadding and backing together traps warmth between the layers. Quilting is not just functional, though, as the patterns of stitches add another facet of decoration. The stitches give a vitality to the design and interesting textures that highlight some areas and throw others into relief. This allows you to manipulate the overall effect to emphasize separate shapes or cross patchwork boundaries and redefine areas of the design. Simple lines forming grids of straight lines or echoing the patchwork and appliqué shapes are often used. However, on one-piece quilts the quilting stitches can really take over. They typically form medallions of stylized floral or shell shapes, providing the main focal points, and the long sinuous curves of stylized feathers or Celtic knots for the borders. Quilting still looks particularly effective on solid, light-coloured fabrics – and this could be a vital factor in your choice of a solid or printed backing fabric.

## QUILTING PATTERNS

The quilts in this book feature a range of quilting ideas that can be achieved without the need for templates or stencils. Some quilts have a design that needs transferring to the fabric, but most have patterns based on simple lines that can be stitched without a pattern. You could choose to use a different pattern to complement your quilt top from the popular ones described here, from traditional single or repeated motifs or, if you feel inspired, you could design your own motif.

Whichever quilting pattern you choose, it is important to decide so that you can mark it out on the quilt top if necessary before you start layering the quilt.

## Straight line quilting

As the name suggests, this quilting pattern uses straight rows of stitches to create lines, squares or diamonds. This cross-hatching is often used as a background filler, which appears to run behind a large quilted or appliquéd motif. This overall pattern tends to make the background recede and allow the motif to dominate.

Straight line quilting is particularly suitable for machine sewing, although it can also be done by hand. If possible, use a quilting foot on the machine. These have a gauge, which you can use to space the lines evenly, working outwards from a central line marked on the quilt top. Alternatively, for hand quilting, or machine quilting with a walking foot, you will need to mark out all the lines. Use the width of a long ruler or cut a long, straight strip of card of the required width to use as a template. Although straight line quilting is usually done with straight stitches, you could also experiment with the automatic or programmed stitches on your machine.

*Straight line quilting*

### In-the-ditch quilting

This type of quilting is stitched along the seam lines or marginally to one side of them. The stitches tend to get hidden, but they do emphasize the patchwork shapes. This can be an advantage, but will leave large puffed up patches of fabric if in-the-ditch quilting is the only form of quilting. However, it is often stitched first to stabilize large areas before working more detailed quilting patterns.

In-the-ditch quilting can be done by hand, but is also a good choice for machine sewing. Feed the work through the machine slowly so that you follow the seam lines accurately. As you sew, gently open up the seam with your hands so that the machine stitches sink in and disappear.

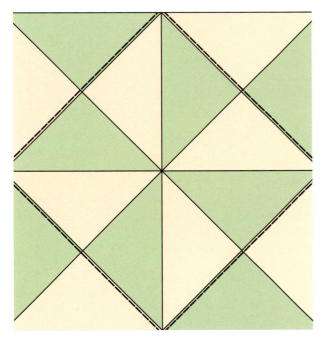

*In-the-ditch quilting*

### Outline quilting

You can use outline quilting to emphasize the design on a patchwork or appliquéd quilt top. A simple line of stitches sewn 6mm (¼in) inside the seam lines, it defines each shape and adds texture to the design without introducing the puffiness that is often characteristic of in-the-ditch quilting.

Ideally, for machine quilting and particularly for curving lines, use a presser foot that will act as an accurate gauge.

Alternatively, and for hand quilting, mark the stitch lines on the quilt top using a quilter's quarter or a quarter wheel against a ruler. You could also use a length of 6mm (¼in) masking tape to act as a gauge for straight lines, but keep using the same strip as you work round the design until it has lost its stickiness and be careful not to stitch through the tape, otherwise you will leave a residue of adhesive that will be difficult to remove.

*Outline quilting*

### Curved line quilting

Also called contour or echo quilting, this is often used to accentuate an appliqué design, which has first been quilted in the ditch. The curved line quilting then radiates out in concentric lines to echo the appliqué shape and fill the background fabric.

To machine sew curved line quilting around simple shapes, use the edge of a walking foot or the gauge on a quilting foot to space the lines. For more complex shapes, mark the lines on the fabric first, then drop the feed dogs on the machine and use a darning foot for free-motion stitching (see page 116). This allows you to move the fabric in any direction to follow the lines. To keep the stitch length regular, feed the work steadily through the machine as it is being stitched.

*Curved line quilting*

## Vermicelli quilting

These small hand or machine stitches meander in random patterns to fill background areas. They flatten the background, while adding interesting detail, and make other areas more prominent. It is ideal for doing on a sewing machine, using a darning foot with the feed dogs dropped (see page 116). Cover the fabric evenly, working small areas at a time and trying not to cross the stitch lines.

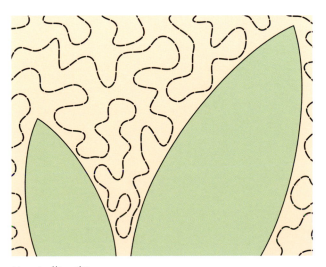

*Vermicelli quilting*

## PREPARING THE FABRICS

After the quilt top has been finished, you may need to mark up the quilting pattern on it. Then the quilt top, wadding and backing fabric need to be basted together.

### Marking up the quilt top

1 Trim any threads off the right side of the quilt top. Square the quilt top up and trim the raw edges. Then press it carefully.

2 Prepare a flat surface for marking out the pattern or design outlines. The quilt top should not slip on the surface, so a table covered with a smooth sheet or a large cutting mat on a table or the floor would be ideal. Place the fabric right side up on the surface.

3 You can trace more complex design outlines onto the right side of the fabric (see page 129). Alternatively, simple patterns such as straight or contour quilting that do not require a design outline can be marked straight onto the quilt top using a sharp quilter's pencil or water-erasable marker and the most appropriate measuring tool.

*Quilter's tip* *Mark the design or pattern with just a broken or dashed line, not a solid line, and only as firmly as you need to see the outline so that there is less of a mark to remove later.*

### Preparing the layers

1 Cut out the fabric for the quilt backing so that it is 5cm (2in) bigger than the quilt top all round. This allowance is for the inevitable take up of fabric during the quilting process. If you are going to have a self binding, add at least another 2.5cm (1in) in addition to the basic allowance.

2 If the finished quilt is wider than the width of the fabric, piece widths together as appropriate to create the required size. If two widths are needed, cut one of them in half lengthways and piece them together on each side of the full width. The resulting two seams will make the backing more durable than one central seam. If three widths are required, position the seams an equal distance from the centre line. Press the seams to one side. Trim the side edges to size after the quilting is completed.

*Piecing the backing together*

③ Cut the wadding so that it is also 5cm (2in) bigger than the quilt top all round. If the wadding is not wide enough, piece lengths together using a large herringbone stitch (see page 113).

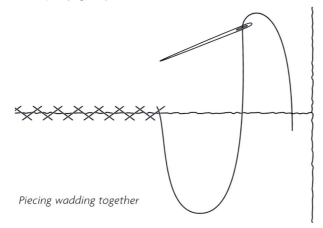

*Piecing wadding together*

④ Find the midpoint along each side of the quilt top and the backing. To find the midpoint on the long sides, align the two short edges, press the fold and insert a pin at each end of the fold. Repeat the process by aligning the long

edges, to find the midpoint on the short sides. Find the midpoints of the wadding in the same way, but just fold and don't press it.

⑤ Tape the backing, wrong side up, to a large flat surface so that it is perfectly flat and taut, but not stretched or distorted. An old table, a large board or even a clean kitchen floor make ideal work surfaces. If you use a good dining table, slip a large cutting mat under the fabric so that you can move it around as you work to protect the surface of the table from needles and pins.

*Quilter's tip* *If the work surface is smaller than the quilt, measure and find the midpoint along each side of the surface. Mark each midpoint by taping a cotton bud or toothpick along the centre line. You can then use these to align with the centre lines of the backing.*

⑥ Centre the wadding on the backing, smoothing it out and aligning the midpoints. Then smooth out the quilt top, right side up, in the centre of the wadding. Make sure that the midpoints are perfectly aligned with those on the wadding and backing.

### Basting the layers together

Use basting stitches (see page 111) to secure the three layers of the quilt together ready for quilting by hand. This is recommended because the stitches can usually be left in place until after the quilting is complete without them getting in the way.

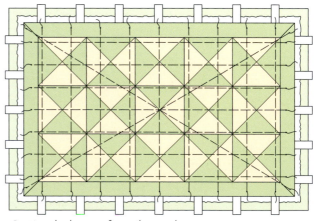

*Basting the layers of a quilt together*

1 Bring a double length of thread, slightly longer than twice the width of the quilt and in a colour to contrast with the fabric, up in the centre of the quilt. Using just half the length of thread, baste a straight line of stitches to just beyond the edge of the quilt top and fasten off the end. Rethread the other end of the thread and baste another line of stitches to just beyond the bottom edge. Continue basting from the horizontal centre line, spacing the basting lines approximately 10cm (4in) apart.

2 Working in the same way, baste from along the vertical centre line. Continue basting until you have a grid of stitch lines, approximately 10cm (4in) apart, radiating out from the centre. Then, if necessary, to make sure that the layers are securely basted together, baste two diagonal lines from corner to corner, crossing in the centre of the quilt.

### Safety pinning the layers together

If you are machine quilting, basting stitches will easily get caught by the needle and so safety pinning the layers together is the better option. Working from the centre of the quilt, use quilter's safety pins to pin along both the vertical and horizontal centre lines. Make sure that you fill the pins with all three layers to stop them slipping and try to

place them in areas that you will not be quilting. Now work out from the centre lines, pinning the layers together every 10cm (4in) to make a grid pattern.

## QUILTING

Quilting by hand produces a softer line of stitches than machine quilting. This is very sympathetic to traditional designs and will give your quilt a real heirloom quality. Although you could quilt on a free-standing frame, a quilting hoop is just as effective and very much more portable. Another traditional hand method that works well for thick quilts, involves simply tying the layers at regular intervals (see hand tying on page 141).

Machine quilting produces a crisp line of regular stitches that look particularly good with modern quilt designs, although a softer effect can still be achieved by using transparent monofilament or closely toning thread. The sewing machine is best suited to quilting straight lines and simple patterns in which the work does not need to be turned too often and a lightweight wadding with less loft is easier to use. Not only is machine quilting much quicker than quilting by hand, but it also withstands constant use and machine washing very well.

### Quilting by hand

1 Place the plain ring of a quilting hoop under the centre of your quilt. Position the ring with the screw over the top of the quilt and the bottom ring. Tighten the screw and the top ring around the bottom ring so that the fabric is slightly less than drum tight and you can pick up a few stitches at a time. You will need both hands for quilting, so it is a good idea to prop the hoop up, for example on the edge of a table.

2 Start at the centre of the quilt and work outwards. Choose as small a needle as you feel comfortable with and thread it with a 45cm (18in) length of thread in a colour to match the quilt top. Knot the end of the thread and take the needle down through the quilt top into the wadding, a short distance from where you intend to start quilting. Bring the needle back up at the starting point. Give the thread a slight tug to pull the knot into the wadding so that the starting point is invisible.

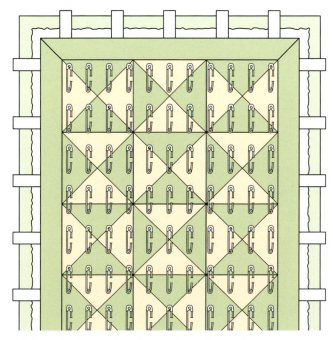

*Safety pinning the three layers of a quilt together*

3 Work with your dominant hand on top of the quilting frame and your other hand beneath. Push the index finger of your lower hand up to make a ridge so that you can follow the stitching line more easily. You may wish to protect this finger with a thimble as well as the middle finger on your upper hand. With practice, your hands will work in unison to a steady rhythm.

4 Work evenly spaced running stitches through all the layers. As you push the needle down through the backing, make contact with the lower index finger and use this to guide the needle back up to the quilt top. As you become more confident, take several stitches onto the needle at once and make smaller, more even stitches. As you work, gently pull the stitches to indent the stitch line evenly. Work stab stitches for the short distance across seams or thicker fabrics.

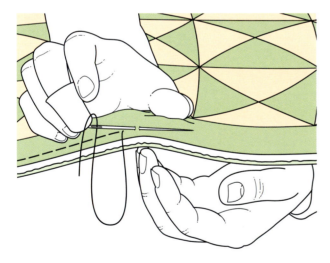

*Forming a slight ridge with the lower index finger to make quilting along the design line easier*

**Quilter's tip** *To quilt round a shape, bring a double length of thread up at the 2 o' clock position. Using just half of the total length of thread, start quilting in one direction. When the first length runs out, rethread the other end and quilt in the other direction. In this way you will always be working comfortably.*

5 When the stitches reach the edge of the hoop, leave the thread hanging or wind it around a pin

so that you can pick it up again later when you move the hoop to the next area. However before you move on, use more thread to complete the rest of the design within the hoop.

6 To move a short distance from one part of the design to another without the thread showing, push the point of the needle through the wadding and bring it up in a new position on the design line.

You can also move across slightly longer distances by taking the point of the needle through the wadding but without pulling the whole needle out of the fabric. Instead, grip the point and swing the eye end round under the fabric to the new point on the design. Carefully bring the needle out eye end first, ready to continue sewing along the new quilting line.

Alternately, move the needle from one quilting line to another by bringing the thread up where it will eventually be hidden under other stitches.

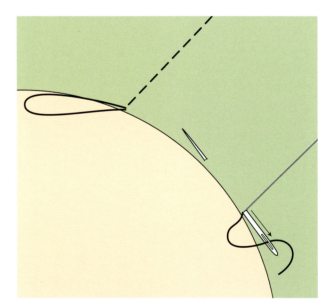

*Threading the needle under the fabric to transfer from one quilting line to another*

7 If you need to quilt up to the edge of the top of the quilt, baste lengths of 20cm (8in) wide cotton fabric to the edges. These extensions will then allow you to centre the edge of the top of the quilt in the hoop and continue quilting.

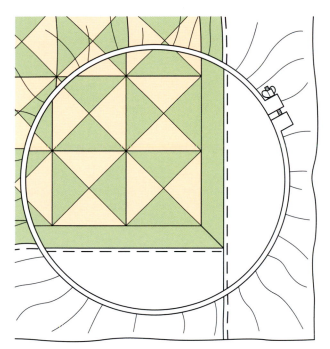

*Adding strips of fabric to the edges of the quilt to make it easier to quilt right up to the edges*

8 To fasten off a thread, first wind it twice round the needle or make a back stitch, splitting the thread of the previous stitch. Then insert the needle through the quilt top into the wadding. Run the needle through the wadding for about 2.5cm (1in), bring it back up to the surface and then carefully trim off the end close to the fabric.

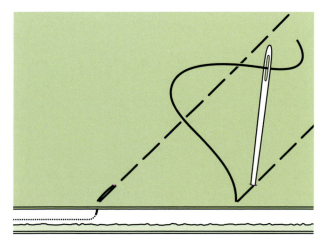

*Fastening off the thread in the wadding layer*

## Tied quilting

1 Assemble the layers of the quilt as usual, but pin or baste them at the points that will be tied together. A heavyweight wadding can be used for this technique. The tying points should be spaced at 7.5–15cm (3–6 in) intervals, depending on how often the quilt will need laundering.

2 Thread a needle with sturdy thread, such as cotton embroidery thread, in a colour to complement or contrast with the fabric. Take the needle down through the layers of the quilt at a tying point, leaving a 5–7.5cm (2–3in) tail on the top. Bring the needle up to the top again and make a back stitch over the tying point through all the layers. Bring the needle up again and take it down at the next tying point. Repeat the process until all the thread has been finished, ending with a completed tie and a 5–7.5cm (2–3in) tail. Complete all the ties in the same way and then cut the threads between each one.

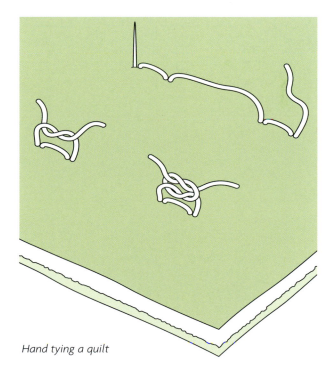

*Hand tying a quilt*

3 Pull each pair of tails to tighten the tie up. Tie each one with a square knot – right over left, left over right – and trim the tails. You could also tie each pair of tails into a bow or trap strands of 5cm (2in) long thread with a second square knot to make a tuft.

### Machine quilting

1 Attach either a walking or a quilting foot to the machine. A quilting foot is useful if you want to use either the foot edge or the attached gauge to space your lines of stitches. However, a walking foot will feed both the quilt top and the backing at an even rate and prevent tucks from forming. Choose a sharp needle to suit the fabric and either a transparent thread or one in a colour to match the quilt top. Set the stitch length at 2 or 3 and loosen the tension of the upper thread slightly.

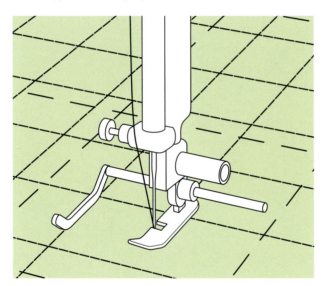

*Quilting with an adjustable gauge*

2 Decide where to start stitching, depending on the quilting pattern. It is often best to start by quilting in the ditch to stabilize the quilt. In this case, start by stitching along the central horizontal axis and then work outwards from there. Then you can go on to quilt specific background areas, again working outwards from the centre.

3 Tightly roll up half of the quilt from one edge and secure it with safety pins or bicycle clips. Fold the bottom edge of the quilt over a few times. Supporting the bottom of the quilt on your knees, slide the rolled edge under the arm of the sewing machine until the starting point is under the needle and the rest of the quilt is on the work surface to the left and behind the machine. The quilt can be rolled up from different directions as quilting progresses.

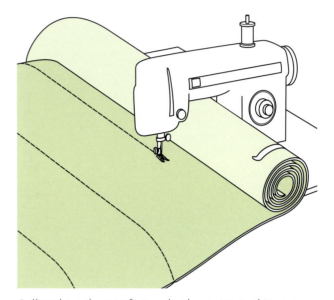

*Rolling the quilt up to fit it under the sewing machine arm*

4 To start at the edge of the quilt, sew a few back stitches or a few stitches on the spot. When you need to start elsewhere, hold a 10cm (4in) length of the top and bottom threads so that they don't tangle and leave them to fasten off later. Stitch slowly so that you can follow the design lines or the gauge accurately. Remove the safety pins as you go, when the layers are securely stitched together. Stitch in the same direction as much as possible given the design so that you have to refold the quilt as little as possible. If you need to stop stitching to reposition the work, insert the needle right into the fabric before raising the foot and pivoting the work.

5 Quilt around the design in as continuous a line as possible, so that you need to start and finish as little as possible. You may need to stitch along the same line more than once to reach different areas of the design, but do this only twice so that the stitches sit neatly on top of each other without creating an ugly line.

6 If a quilting line finishes at the edge of the quilt, fasten off with a few back stitches or a few stitches on the spot. To fasten off both the starting and finishing threads elsewhere on the quilt, pull each top thread to the backing side and knot it with the matching bottom thread. Thread the pair into a needle. Insert the needle into the wadding, bring it up again 2.5cm (1in) away and trim it off.

# Finishing the quilt

Traditionally, quilts are finished around the edges with a narrow binding, which can either match or contrast with the fabrics on the quilt top. A strong binding secures the edges of all three layers, giving the quilt stability and increasing its life. The binding is often the part of a quilt to wear first, but fortunately is also the easiest part to replace.

After all the hard work you have invested in your quilt, you might like to incorporate your name and a few other details in the design or on the back. You might even be tempted to make a sleeve so that you can display your quilt on a wall, rather than putting it to work on a bed. Either way, you will need to look after it well so that you can appreciate your stylish decorative statement or future heirloom for many years to come.

It is advisable to cut the lengths of fabric for the binding only once the quilting has been completed, when the exact dimensions of the quilt top can be accurately measured. Base the binding on the measurements across the midpoints of the quilt top and ease the edges to fit.

## ATTACHING BINDINGS

### Square binding

This strong binding is made with four strips of fabric. The top and bottom strips overlap the side strips at the corners.

1 Trim all three layers of the quilt so that the edges are straight and the corners are square. Put a pin at the midpoint along each edge and measure across the middle of the quilt from pin to opposite pin to give you the basic length and width for the binding strips.

2 To make a binding approximately 2cm (³⁄₄in) wide, cut four 5cm (2in) strips of fabric on the straight or cross grain. The two strips for the sides must each be the exactly as long as the finished quilt top. The strips for the top and bottom must be as long as the width of the quilt top, plus 5cm (2in). Press a 6mm (¼in) turning along one long edge of each strip.

3 Align the raw edge of one of the longer strips along one long edge of the quilt and pin them, right sides together. Sew the binding in place with a 6mm (¼in) seam.

Turn the binding over along the edge of the quilt and slip stitch it in place. Attach the other long strip to the opposite side of the quilt in the same way.

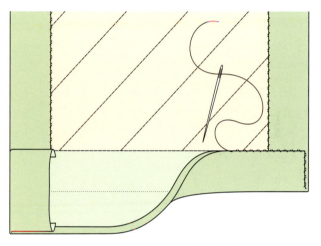

*Stitching the bottom edge of a square binding in place*

4 Sew one of the shorter strips to the bottom edge of the quilt with the first seam, making sure there is the same amount of excess binding at each end. Turn the ends of the excess binding over each corner and pin them in place. Then turn the binding over along the edge of the quilt top and slip stitch it in place. Attach the other short strip to the top edge of the quilt in the same way.

### Double binding

Double binding is made from one long strip of fabric, which is mitred at each corner of the quilt and forms the strongest type of binding. The finished binding will be about 12mm (½in) wide.

1 Trim all three layers of the quilt the same as for a square binding. Cut 6.5cm (2 ½in) strips of fabric on the straight or cross grain. Next sew the strips together so that you have enough binding to go round the total perimeter of the quilt, with an additional 50cm (20in) as well. Press the strip in half lengthways, wrong sides together. Press 6mm (¼in) under on one short end of the strip to make the starting end.

*Quilter's tip* **In order** *to avoid any excess fabric at the corners that would be caused by seams in the binding, do a trial run before you decide where to start attaching the binding.*

2 With right sides together, start to pin the raw edges of the binding along one edge of the quilt, about 25cm (10in) from the corner. Beginning 10cm (4in) from the starting end of the binding, machine sew along the pinned edge with a 6mm (¼in) seam, up to 6mm (¼in) away from the adjacent edge. Fasten off and cut the thread, and remove the quilt from the machine.

3 Place the quilt right side up on a flat surface. Lift and fold the binding so that it stretches away from the quilt, but in a straight line with the next edge of the quilt to be stitched. Pin that fold across the corner to hold it in place if you wish.

*Making the first fold at the corner of the double binding*

4 Lift the binding again and align the raw edge along the next edge of the quilt to be stitched. Make sure that the small tuck at the corner stays in place and that the exposed fold aligns with the stitched edge of the quilt. Pin the binding in place to within 6mm (¼in) of the next corner. Machine sew along the edge, starting and finishing 6mm (¼in) from each corner.

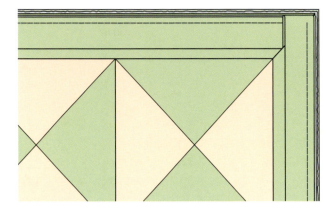

*Stitching the second edge of the binding in place*

5 Repeat this process until you have stitched the border all round the quilt to within 10cm (4in) of the starting point. Fasten off the thread and remove the quilt from the machine. Measure the remaining length of binding up to the starting end and cut it, adding 1cm (½in) extra. Tuck this end into the starting end. Pin and sew the ends in place.

6 Fold the binding to the back of the quilt to cover the raw edges and pin it in place. Make a 45 degree fold at each of the corners to match the mitred corners on the front of the quilt. Slip stitch the edges and corners in place on the back of the quilt, taking care not to let the stitches go through to the front.

## PERSONALIZING YOUR QUILT

Many quilters hope that their quilts will be prized by future generations of family or friends, who will be interested to know their name and other details about the quilt. So take pride in your quilt and record at least your name, the name of the quilt and the date it was finished. You will be following a great tradition. You can either incorporate these details in the design itself or make a patch to go on the back of the quilt.

Cut a patch of fabric that will match or contrast with the backing fabric and add your details with a permanent marker. Alternatively, you could embroider your details onto the fabric, design your label on the computer and feed the fabric through the printer on freezer paper or use some of the other creative methods used on the quilts in this book. Slip stitch the patch in place on the back of the quilt, taking care not to allow the stitches to go through to the front.

## MAKING A HANGING SLEEVE

You can display your quilt on a wall if you make one or more hanging sleeves through which to slip a pole. The ends of the sleeves should be no closer than 2.5cm (1in) from the side edges of the quilt and the pole should be 5cm (2in) shorter than the width of the quilt so that it does not show from the front.

1 Cut one strip of 20cm (8in) wide fabric, 2.5cm (1in) longer than the width of the quilt. Divide this strip into shorter lengths if you would prefer to make two or three sleeves across the top of a large quilt.

2 Fold the fabric in half lengthways, wrong sides together, and sew the long edges together. Press the seam and then the sleeve with the seam centred on the wrong side. Fold the short edges under and slip stitch a hem on each.

3 Pin one long fold of the sleeve to the back of the quilt just below the top edge of the binding. Slip stitch the fold in place through the backing and the wadding, but do not allow the stitches to show through on the quilt top. Then pin and slip stitch the opposite edge of the sleeve in place, allowing room to fit a pole through the sleeve.

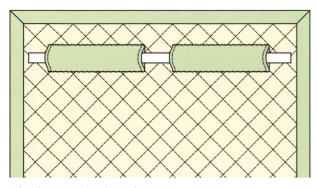

*The sleeves and pole in place*

## TAKING CARE OF YOUR QUILT

Whether you display your quilt on a bed, sofa or wall, if you look after it properly it will stay in good condition for many years. Keep it out of strong, direct sunlight as this will fade the colours and away from damp, which will cause mildew.

The occasional good shake may be all that is needed to remove dust and fluff up the wadding. To clean a fragile quilt, lay it right side up on a flat surface. Put a layer of net or muslin (cheesecloth) over the top and peg it in place. Vacuum away any loose dust, holding the nozzle above the surface.

### Laundering

Wash a quilt only if you have already pre-shrunk the fabrics and ensured that they are colour fast. If that is not the case or you have used delicate fabrics, have your quilt dry-cleaned instead.

1 Whether you wash the quilt in a machine or by hand, use only warm water. Even a mild washing detergent is best avoided. If you are washing a quilt by hand, the bath may be the best and most convenient place. Make sure you gently squeeze all the water out of the quilt and then roll it up in towels which will remove as much moisture as possible.

2 If you want to wash your quilt in the machine, use a setting to suit all three layers. A short spin will take out much of the moisture, but do not tumble dry the quilt.

3 Hang the quilt on a washing line on a windy, but not very hot, day, but only if it is not too heavy and can be well supported along its whole length, to avoid it pulling out of shape and the quilting threads breaking. Otherwise lay it on a flat outdoor surface – such as the lawn, patio or a trampoline – between two clean sheets.

### Storage

Fold and roll your quilt up in a clean sheet or place it in a clean pillowcase, both of which will allow it to breathe. Avoid storing it in plastic as this will encourage mildew. Once a year air the quilt outdoors. Then fold the quilt along different lines and return it to storage.

### Repairing quilts

It is easy to repair unravelled stitches or worn bindings, which are the parts of a quilt that usually wear first. If you need to repair stitches, put the quilt in a quilting hoop and carefully unpick the stitches to a point where they can be fastened off. Then replace them with new stitches. To replace a binding, first distress enough fabric to make a replacement by washing it repeatedly or fading it in the sun to the extent that it matches the character of the quilt. Carefully remove the original binding and attach the new one.

# Templates

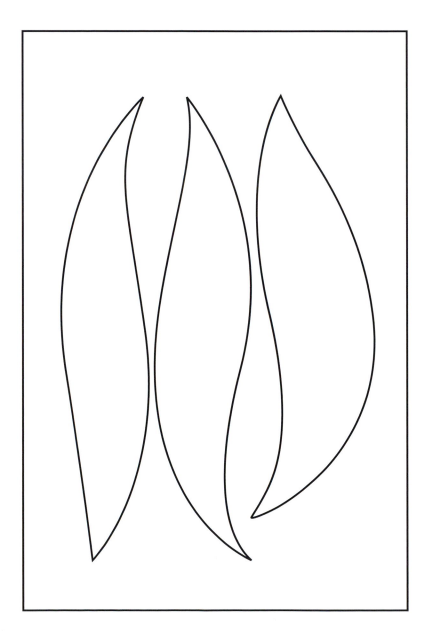

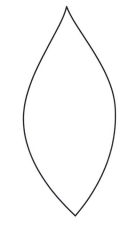

**ABOVE: POPPY FIELDS**

The leaf template is actual size.


**OPPOSITE: POPPY FIELDS**

Enlarge the design so that the outline measures 150 x 185cm (59 x 72³⁄₄in).

**GUMLEAVES**

The leaf template is actual size.

**ABOVE: SPIRIT OF NDEBELE**

Enlarge the design so that the outline
measures 81 x 120cm (32 x 48in).

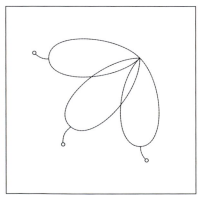

**LIBERTY'S SONG BIRD**

Enlarge the design for the corner post
to 200%.

**OPPOSITE: LIBERTY'S SONG
BIRD**

Enlarge the design so that the outline
measures 80 x 100cm (32 x 40in).

## WHITE ROMANCE

Enlarge these templates for the top and bottom borders to 250%. Join the two parts, overlapping the red sections. Then trace a reverse image of the whole template and match the two new parts by overlapping the blue section.

## WHITE ROMANCE

Enlarge these templates for the side borders to 250%. Join the two parts, overlapping the red sections. Then trace the whole template again, rotate it 180 degrees and match the two new parts by overlapping the blue section.

## GUARDIAN ANGELS

Enlarge all the templates to 200%.

6

*Cut 2*
*(Cut 2 in reverse)*

5

*Cut 2*
*(Cut 2 in reverse)*

3

*Cut 2*
*(Cut 2 in reverse)*

## MACHIKO'S GIFT

Enlarge these two templates to 800%. Arrange the enlarged templates with a gap of approximately 6.5cm (2$\frac{1}{2}$in) between them.

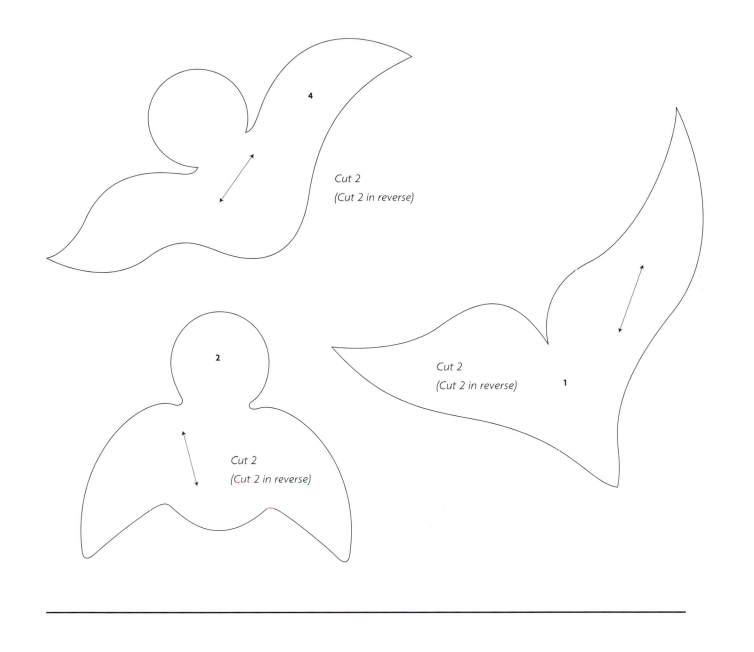

**4**

Cut 2
(Cut 2 in reverse)

**1**

Cut 2
(Cut 2 in reverse)

**2**

Cut 2
(Cut 2 in reverse)

**MACHIKO'S GIFT**
Enlarge all the templates to 200%.

# Contributors

Machiko's gift

**Hiroko Aono-Billson** studied textile design at Central Saint Martin's College of Art & Design in London. After her studies, she started designing her own range of products, which she sold from a stall in Portobello Road. She then went on to launch *Blue field* as a label in 1997. Having recently returned to Japan, Hiroko is rediscovering traditional Japanese crafts and is incorporating their influences into her new ranges. Hiroko's work reflects her love of detail, with designs and hand-sewn motifs inspired by plants, leaves and flowers. Her products have been featured in publications such as *The Guardian*, *Homes and Gardens*, *Marie Claire* and *Vogue*.

Gumleaves

**Jan Clark** has used textiles to express her inner voice for most of her life and art quilts have been the main vehicle for that expression since 1998. At that time her inspiration came from the magnificent landscapes around her in northwest America. When she returned to her native Australia, she began to focus on the minutiae of the vegetation, pebbles and insects in the forests and rockpools near her home in the Hunter Valley. Although not always recognizable, these elements are now the subjects of her textile art. Jan hopes her work expresses her joy in the natural world and the gumleaves that she scatters throughout it symbolize her feeling of being where she belongs. Jan's work has been exhibited in Australia, Europe, New Zealand and North America.

Forms of attachment

**Diane Groenewegen** was born in Sydney. Educated in Australia, she trained and practised as an art teacher before becoming a freelance textile artist. She now conducts workshops all over Australia and writes for art journals and magazines. Diane's quilts often include printing and hand embroidery. As a collector of textiles, buttons and vintage costumes, her inspiration often comes from her love of antique textiles, which she likes to infuse with a new lease of life by incorporating them in her quilts. Diane's work is represented in the Queensland Art Gallery and in many private collections in Australia, Europe and the United States.

Cocoon

**Gillian Hand** began the journey into contemporary textile arts after discovering traditional patchwork and quilting. She soon diverged into experimental contemporary quilt making and art-to-wear garments. Gillian often draws her inspiration from nature and particularly from strong textures and patterns, in rich and variegated colours. She is fascinated by the idea that we are all connected in the 'greater scheme of things' and her work reflects this sense of wholeness. She is currently exploring the themes of unity, diversity and contrast, especially in the relationships between the natural elements and all living beings. Gillian developed *faux-felt* through experimentation with natural fibres. She has won several awards for her faux-felt designs and enjoys teaching workshops in this technique.

Bejewelled seams

**Esther MacFarlane** has been drawing, painting and sewing since she was a small child. For years sewing had a purely practical purpose of making clothes and home furnishings. More recently, Esther has had more time to extend her needle skills for her own enjoyment and expression. She loves the tactile nature of textile art and the fabrics often inspire her designs. While she appreciates cottons for their simplicity, she is particularly drawn to luxurious fabrics, with their rich colours and textures. She is especially intrigued by the way a quilt develops from conception to birth – sometimes most of the elements can be apparent at the outset, but often they are only revealed stage by stage.

Pompom maze

**Hikaru Noguchi** comes from Japan and a family that has long connections with textiles and related crafts. She trained as a graphic designer and then moved to England in 1989 to study constructed textiles at Middlesex University. After finishing her studies, she began to design fabrics for furnishings and garments, specializing in tactile knitted, woven and quilted constructions. Her distinctive style has won her commissions for furnishing fabrics from all over the world and her garments and fashion accessories are sold in Europe, Japan and the United States. Hikaru travels widely and draws her inspiration from craftspeople working in isolated rural locations, rather than urban design. These same people are often employed to make the items that she has designed, keeping local crafts alive, while introducing new ideas and techniques.

Cappuccino waves

**Angelina Pieroni** has always been passionate about textiles and the way they can be manipulated to make them into three-dimensional objects. She originally trained in theatre costume and feels privileged to have worked with incredible fabrics and some of the top designers, whilst making costumes for the film, opera and ballet industries for fifteen years. Eventually, having children gave Angelina the opportunity to put into practice all the ideas she had stored away for years – including those for designing and making quilts.

Spirit of Ndebele

**Terry Pryke** was born and now lives in Johannesburg, where she attended art school before working as a display artist. After the birth of her daughter, she started her own company and now runs a successful business creating floral art for weddings and corporate functions. Her love of flowers and colour is often reflected in her needlework. She inherited her skill and love for sewing from her grandmother who, like Terry, was rarely seen without some kind of needlework in her hands. She sees any spare time as an opportunity to create something new – the quilt, Spirit of Ndebele, was made in the passenger seat on a 6000km road trip across Africa! Terry has won several awards for her work and has had quilts commissioned from as far away as Germany and the United Kingdom.

Earthspring

**Alison Schwabe's** love of textile art began with an embroidery class in 1976 and her early work was inspired by her native Australian landscape. However, a move to the United States in 1987 introduced her to quilt making and she began to explore non-traditional techniques and the potential for self expression in this art form. With an academic background in geography and ancient civilisations, Alison found much to interest her in the manmade painted, chipped or carved primal markings in the landscape of southwest America. More recently, her inspiration has come from landscape patterns and textures. Alison has contributed to various magazines and books, and her quilt art has been exhibited in Australia, Europe, Japan, the United Kingdom, Uruguay and the United States.

Oxfam flowers

**Karen Spurgin** was a tutor in the textile department at the Royal College of Art in London before becoming a freelance textile designer. Most of her current design work is for fashion, but also includes fabrics for the film, television and interiors industries. Her work has included designs for the film *Topsy Turvy*, which won an Oscar for costumes. Karen was originally drawn to quilt making through her love of abstract art, having read that the painters were often influenced by quilt designs. She then realised how much she sympathized with the ideas of recycling fabric to make something both useful and beautiful, and of passing quilts down to future generations. Karen now loves designing large-scale quilts, which incorporate treasured scraps of fabric and ribbon.

**Karen Hemingway** is a freelance writer and editor. She wrote the tools, materials and techniques sections of this book and would particularly like to acknowledge the advice of Linda Kerswill of The Cotton Club, Bampton, UK, which was invaluable in the preparation of this text. Karen started sewing as a young girl and since then has always found time to squeeze a broad range of needlework and other related crafts into life outside work. She particularly enjoys any opportunity to combine her love of all things textile and her professional skills with words.

# Index

Page numbers in *italics* refer to illustrations

adhesives, 9, 131
Aono-Billson, Hiroko, *47*, 95, 156
appliqué, 117, 128–34
    calculating yardage, 106
    projects, 22, 46, 50, 54, 66, 86, 98
appliqué foot, 115
Art Deco abstract, 26–29, *27*

back stitch, 46, 111
back stitch knot, 110
backing, 16, 107, 137
baking parchment, 134
basting, 111, 115, 138
batting see wadding
beading, 68
bed quilts
    measuring for, 106
    projects, 22, 26, 30, 34, 42, 46, 50,
        58 70, 78, 82, 94, 98
beeswax, 12
Bejewelled seams, 42–5, *43*
bias, cutting on, 107, 108, 109, 119, 131
bindings, 16, 108, 143–4, 145
borders, 107, 126–7
buttonhole stitch, 134

Cappuccino waves, 90–3, *91*
card, 9, 129
care of quilts, 145
chain piecing, 48, 125
chalk powder wheels, 11
charm squares, 84
Clark, Jan, *51*, 156
cleaning quilts, 145
clear plastic foot, 115
close satin stitch, 115
Cocoon, 62–5, *63*
colour fast fabrics, 109, 145
colour schemes, 17–18
contour quilting 56, 69, 136
corners, mitring, 36–7, 126–7
corners, turning, 115, 133, 134

cot quilt, 54
craft knives, 9
cross stitch, 73, 112
cross-hatch patterns, 69, 103, 135
curved line quilting, 56, 69, 136
curved seams, 44, 124–5, 126
curved shapes, 118, 131, 134
cut-and-sew technique, 44, 78, 80
cutting equipment, 10
cutting mats, 10

darning foot, 13, 116, 137
decorative cross stitch, 88
Desert dreaming, 86–9, *87*
designs, transfer of, 8, 128–9
detergents, avoidance of, 109, 145
distressing fabric, 145
double binding, 143–4
drafting triangles, 8, 109
dressmaker's scissors, 10, 120
dyeing fabrics, 62

Earthspring, 78–81, *79*
echo quilting, 56, 69, 136
embroidery
    pressing, 117
    projects, 30, 34, 60, 72, 82, 86, 96, 100
    stitches, 112–13, 116
embroidery hoops, 12, 116, 131

fabric paints, 62
fabrics, 15–19
    cutting, 120–2
    preparing, 109
fat eighths, 15
fat quarters, 15
faux felt, 62, 157
finger pressing, 117
finishing techniques, 143–5
fixing dye, 62, 109
flexi-curve, 11
fly stitch, 60, 112
Forms of attachment, 70–3, *71*
free-motion stitching, 13, 116

projects, 52, 64, 96
freezer paper, 10, 130, 145
French knots, 30, 60, 97, 112
French knots on navy, 30–3, *31*
fringing, 86, 88
fusible web, 10, 130–1, 134

geometric shapes, cutting, 120–1
glue sticks, 9, 131
grain, of fabric, 109
greaseproof paper, 8, 129
grid method of enlargement, 128
Groenewegen, Diane, *71*, *87*, 156
Guardian angels, 58–61, *59*
Gumleaves, 50–3, *51*

half-square triangles, 48, 122
hand appliqué, 129–33
hand piecing, 123–5
hand quilting, 140–2
hand sewing, 110–14
hand tying, 30, 96, 142
    projects, 32, 102
Hand, Gillian, *63*, 156
hanging sleeves, 145
herringbone stitch, 34, 88, 113
hoops, 12, 116, 131, 140–1

in-the-ditch quilting, 136
interfacing, 10, 130
irons, 12

laundering quilts, 145
Liberty's song bird, 46–9, *47*
light boxes, 11, 129
lint, removal of, 56

Machiko's gift, 94–7, *95*
machine appliqué, 130–4
machine piecing, 125–7
machine quilting, 139, 140, 142
machine sewing, 110, 114–16
marking out fabric, 11, 119, 129, 137
masking tape, 13, 136

McFarlane, Esther, *43*, *55*, 156
measuring equipment, 10
mitred corners, 36–7, 126–7
monofilament quilting thread, 14, 140

nap, aligning, 119
needle threaders, 12, 110
needleturning allowances, 132, 133
needles, 12, 13, 110
Noguchi, Hikaru, *39*, *75*, 157

outline quilting, 56, 136
Oxfam flowers, 82–95, *83*

patchwork, 118–27
  border, 46
  projects, 26, 34, 38, 42, 46, 70, 74,
    78, 82, 86, 94
  yardage, 106–7
patterns
  appliqué, 128–9
  quilting, 135–7
pencils, 8, 11
permanent marker pens, 8, 118, 145
personalising quilts, 144
piecing patchwork, 123–7
Pieroni, Angelina, *23*, *91*, 157
pins, 11, 114, 120
Pompom maze, 38–41, *39*
pompoms, making, 40
Poppy fields, 98–103, *99*
pre-shrinking fabrics, 109
presser foot, 13, 136
pressing, 117
printing fabric, 70, 72
Pryke, Terry, *67*, *99*, 157

quarter wheels, 11, 119, 136
quarter-square triangles, 48, 122, 124
quilter's pencils, 11
quilter's quarters, 11, 119, 136
quilter's rulers, 10
quilting, 135–42
quilting foot, 13, 135, 142

quilting gauges, 142
quilting hoops, 12, 140–1

rectangles, cutting, 121
registration marks, 118, 124
repairing quilts, 145
reverse appliqué, 50
reversing shapes, 119, 129
ribbons, 34, 37, 72
Rose constellations, 22–5, *23*
rotary cutters, 8, 10, 120–1
rotary cutting, 42, 44, 78
rulers, 8, 10
running foot *see* presser foot
running stitch, 34, 110–11, 115, 130

safety pins, 13, 142
sashes, 106, 107
Schwabe, Alison, *79*, 157
scissors, 9, 10, 12, 120
Sea of dreams, 34–7, *35*
seam allowances, 117, 118, 119, 122, 124,
  125
seam gauges, 114
seam rippers, 13, 116
seams, 117, 125–6
selvedges, 109
sewing machines, 13
shrinkage, 106, 109
slip stitch, 112
Spirit of Ndebele, 66–9, *67*
Spurgin, Karen, *27*, *31*, *35*, *59*, *83*, 157
square binding, 143
square knots, 141
squares, cutting, 121
stab stitch, 111, 140
stains, removal of, 24, 44, 93
star stitch, 49, 113
starching fabric, 109
stay stitches, 133
stitches, 110–13, 115–16, 151
storage of quilts, 145
straight edges, 109
straight line quilting, 135

straight seams, 123–4, 125
straight-cornered borders, 126
strip piecing, 82, 85

tacking *see* basting
tape measures, 10
Tasselbrick, 74–7, *75*
tassels, making, 76, 97
template plastic, 8, 118, 129
templates, 8–9, 126–7, 128–9
tension, 110, 114, 142
thimbles, 12, 110, 140
threads, 14
  length, 110, 139
  securing, 110, 134, 139, 140, 142
throws, 16, 74, 90
tied quilting, 96, 150
tonal values, 17
tools, 8–13
tracing designs, 8, 129
tracing paper, 8
turning allowances, 129, 130, 131, 133

vacuuming quilts, 145
vermicelli quilting, 64, 137
vermicelli stitch, 116

wadding, 14–15, 138
walking foot, 13, 135, 136, 142
wall-hangings, 16, 62, 66, 86, 144–5
washing quilts, 145
water-erasable markers, 11, 119, 138
water-soluble adhesives, 9, 133
water-soluble fabric, 64, 65
waxed paper *see* greasproof paper
weave, of fabric, 16, 109
whipped back stitch, 113, 102
whipped spider's web, 113, 102
White romance, 58–61, *59*
work surfaces, 138

yardage, estimating, 106–7

zigzag foot, 115

**UK Publisher:** Catie Ziller

**Project Editor:** Karen Hemingway

**Additional editorial work:** JMS Books LLP

**Designer:** Helen Taylor

**Photographer:** Paola Pieroni

**Stylist:** Ali Allen

**Illustrator:** Stephen Dew

**Indexer:** Vanessa Speller

© Marabout (Hachette Livre), 2004
This edition published by Hachette Illustrated UK,
Octopus Publishing Group Ltd., 2–4 Heron Quays, London E14 4JP

A CIP catalogue for this book is available from the British Library

ISBN-13: 978-1-84430-112-6

ISBN-10: 1-84430-112-5

Printed by Toppan Printing Co., (HK) Ltd.

10 9 8 7 6 5 4